SHIPWRECKS
OF SUSSEX

SHIPWRECKS
OF SUSSEX

Wendy Hughes

The
History
Press

First published 2011

The History Press
The Mill, Brimscombe Port
Stroud, Gloucestershire, GL5 2QG
www.thehistorypress.co.uk

British Library Cataloguing in Publication Data.
A catalogue record for this book is available from the British Library.

ISBN 978 0 7524 6010 9

Typesetting and origination by The History Press
Printed in Great Britain

CONTENTS

ABOUT THE AUTHOR

Wendy Hughes turned to writing in 1989 when ill health and poor vision forced her into early medical retirement. Since then she has published twenty-six non-fiction books and over 1,700 articles, on a variety of subjects. Her work has appeared in magazines as diverse as *The Lady*, *Funeral Service Journal*, *On the Road*, *3rd Stone*, *Celtic Connections*, *Best of British* and *Guiding*.

Wendy has spent many years campaigning and writing on behalf of people affected by Stickler Syndrome, a progressive genetic connective tissue disorder from which she herself suffers. She founded the Stickler Syndrome Support Group and raises awareness of the condition amongst the medical profession, and produces the group's literature.

She also talks and instructs on the craft of writing, is membership secretary for the Society of Women Writers and Journalists, and is a member of the Society of Authors.

ACKNOWLEDGEMENTS

So many people helped me with the research for this book, and if I have inadvertently forgotten to include your name, please accept my apologies and sincere thanks for your assistance.

My thanks to:

Conrad Hughes, my husband, for chauffeuring, taking so many photographs and for his skilful editing of the final draft, thus saving me from publishing too many silly mistakes.

Peter Bailey, of the Newhaven Local and Maritime Museum, for his help with Newhaven shipwrecks, especially his expert knowledge on HMS *Brazen*, and for the use of photographs taken by Conrad Hughes at the museum.

Arthur Smith, of the Newhaven Local and Maritime Museum, for his willingness to locate information, and provide me with photocopies.

Sue Sutton, and various members of the staff at Seaford Museum and Heritage Society, for their help, and for making their archives freely available to me, as well as allowing me to use many of their photographs.

Hayden Luke, Independent Museum and Education Consultant, and trustee of the Nautical Museum Trust, part of the Shipwreck Heritage Museum, Hastings, for his willingness in making available several videos to watch at the museum, and for allowing me to use archive photographs as well as those taken by Conrad Hughes at the Museum.

David Renno, author of two excellent books on nineteenth-century wrecks (see Bibliography) and trustee of the Nautical Museum Trust, part of the Shipwreck Heritage Museum, Hastings, for his guidance towards several books and newspaper articles, and for images of several ships that were wrecked at Hastings.

Martin Hayes and the library staff at Worthing Library for their constant help and friendly service.

West Sussex Past Pictures website (www.westsussexpast.org.uk), which has over 11,500 images of the area, and to Martin Hayes who allowed me to use several archive photographs in this book.

Steve Webster, Senior Project Manager (coastal and marine), Wessex Archaeology for sharing the report on the *Thomas Lawrence* with me, and for giving me permission to use the information in this book.

Janet Cameron, who helped locate information concerning the shipwreck of SS *Brussels*.

James Thatcher, Marlipins Museum, Shoreham-by-Sea, who allowed me to photograph items at the museum, and to use some archive photographs from the West Sussex Past website in this book.

Sean Dwane, Sales/Marketing Manager of Hammerpot Brewery, for information and allowing me to use the bottle label for Bottle Wreck Porter. (www.hammerpot-brewery.co.uk)

Tony Daly (www.coastguardsofyesteryear.org), who provided information on coastguards and allowed me to use the coastguard and breeches buoy photographs.

Divers David Ronnan and Sylvia Pryer, of Dive 125 (www.dive125.co.uk), for allowing me to use the image of a plate recovered from the SS *Seaford* containing the London, Brighton & South Coast Railway logo.

Last but certainly not least, my commissioning editor Amy Rigg at The History Press, for bringing this book safely through to publication.

INTRODUCTION

THE SEA, in all her moods, has always held a fascination for me, and one of my earliest childhood memories includes ships. Born and brought up in Swansea, South Wales, every New Year's Eve I would climb Kilvey Hill with my father and watch the big ships and the tugs in Swansea Docks, hooting and sending firecrackers into the air as everyone cheered and welcomed in the New Year. As I grew older I became fascinated with the Gower Peninsula, with its thrilling stories of smuggling and wrecking, and tales of the ships that went down in the rocky waters around the Peninsula. Upon moving to the Worthing area, a stone's throw from the sea, I read the stories concerning a seafaring, fishing and smuggling community with great interest, and approached the subject of Shipwrecks in Sussex with the renewed enthusiasm of childhood, as I uncovered one enthralling story after another.

The coastline covered is this book is from Chichester in West Sussex through to Rye in East Sussex, and in such a small book it would be impossible to highlight the 4,000 or more ships that went down in these waters, sometimes referred to as 'the diver's paradise'. When I started researching shipwrecks for this book, it soon became evident that I would need to be selective, very selective indeed. If only we could roll back the sea, what treasures we would find, on a seabed littered with wrecks that, over a period of time, have become tangled with parts from one wreck intermingling with another and all with a unique tale to tell. Today with diving becoming an increasingly popular leisure activity, and dedicated marine archaeologists who are interested in discovering the past, slowly the sea is giving up her secrets.

To mention all the ships that went down in these waters would take several volumes, and could be divided into many interesting categories; in fact this book went through a number of rewrites as I shifted chapters around, moved some ships to other chapters, and deleted some chapters completely. Two chapters I purposely took out concerned the vast trade in smuggling and deliberate wrecking along the Sussex coast. I found this is a fascinating subject for another subject book, and felt that I could not do justice to it in this book concerning shipwrecks. I have also only mentioned a minute number of the ships that were lost through enemy action during both world wars, because again this is an immense subject, and one that deserves a book of its own.

Some of the most spectacular shipwrecks occurred around the cliffs at Seven Sisters, and at Newhaven, Seaford and Beachy Head, because here the magnificent cliffs are at their most dangerous and coupled with unpredictable currents and south-westerly winds catching many an unsuspecting experienced sailor by surprise, it is little wonder that so many ships came to grief along this stretch. Some of the most famous wrecks included in this book are the loss of the *Anne* in 1690, during the Battle of Beachy Head, a story that even includes deliberate destroying of the ship, as well as mutiny on board. The wreck of the *Nympha Americana* in 1747 brought out the worst in residents as they looted anything they could lay their hands on. The *Amsterdam*, on her maiden voyage, also went down in 1747 and, since she was discovered in 1969, has revealed some interesting artefacts and provided us with incredible tales of pilfering, even from the houses where soldiers were billeted. One of the saddest stories must be that of Newhaven's biggest maritime disaster when 109 were lost on HMS *Brazen* in 1800, captained by James Hanson, who sailed the world with Edward Vancouver only to lose his life so near to our shores. In more recent times the discovery of a tombstone on board a wreck led to the identification of the *Thomas Lawrence* that went down in 1862, providing us with the sad tale of Julia Adriane Jahncke and her baby son Franz, as well as revealing a fascinating cargo of muskets, machetes and bottles of wine and perfume. It is thanks to such excellent museums such as the Shipwreck Heritage Museum, Hastings, Seaford Museum and Heritage Society, Newhaven Maritime Museum and Marlipins Museum at Shoreham-by-Sea that these stories are kept alive as they are researched and updated, so that future generations can appreciate the dilemmas these sailing ships and seamen found themselves in without the aid of today's navigational equipment, and help us to appreciate the sacrifices these mariners made to bring trade to our shores.

Further along the coast we read of the bravery of the crew on the lifeboat *Mary Stanford* who, in 1928, lost their lives going to the aid of the *Alice of Riga*. A large memorial in Rye harbour fittingly states, 'We have done that which was our duty to do'. The mariners and fishermen of Worthing also considered it a duty to risk their lives to save others, and here eleven brave men lost their lives, making nine women widows and forty-seven children fatherless, when their boat capsized going to the aid of the *Lalla Rookh*.

The choice of shipwrecks is entirely mine and I hope that readers will each find something of interest and be inspired enough to visit the maritime museums around the coast to learn more about this fascinating subject.

Wendy Hughes, Rustington, 2011

One

EARLY WRECKS

BEFORE THE nineteenth century there were no newspapers, radio or even television reports to inform us that a ship had been wrecked, and with poor communications it would have taken many months before families knew the fate of their loved one, if at all. Some wrecks only became known when bodies were washed ashore, or in modern times, thanks to divers discovering a wreck. Reports of the earliest ships known to have floundered along the Sussex coast are sketchy, although a few are well documented, and I will attempt to highlight those that we know a little about, or have an interesting story to tell, but this is only the tip of the iceberg of what lies deep beneath the sea along the South Coast.

The earliest known wrecks along the Sussex coast are the *Marie* of Santander, wrecked in 1368, and a Dutch ship in 1617, both around the Birling Gap area. The latter was only known because the Dutch East India Company lodged documentation in the Admiralty Court archives for the recovery of the cargo. Records also show that a twenty-four-gun Spanish warship, *St James*, ran aground at Heene, near Worthing, in January 1644 but was successfully refloated, and sailed on to London with its cargo before being returned to its owners.

One of the best documented early wrecks is that of the British warship *Anne*, lost during the Battle of Beachy Head in 1690. She was built by King Charles II, launched at Chatham in 1678, and named after Princess Anne (1665-1714). She was a magnificent ship, armed with seventy guns, and one of Samuel Pepys' standard warships, of which thirty were built. The events leading up to the loss of the *Anne* began in 1688 when James II fled from England, and William of Orange and his wife Mary claimed the English throne. William had always been an enemy of Louis XIV of France and his success at gaining the throne of England made war inevitable. This resulted in the famous Battle of Beachy Head in 1690 and victory for France, but certainly not a great

Grenades, cannonballs and musket balls recovered from the *Anne* in 1974. (Conrad Hughes, by kind permission of the Shipwreck Heritage Centre, Hastings)

one. The Anglo-Dutch fleet only lost one ship in the battle, although several ships were deliberately scuppered to prevent them falling into French hands.

The French fleet, under Tourville, had seventy-three ships and eighteen fire ships and a total of 4,703 pieces of cannon. On the other side the English could only muster thirty-five ships and six fire ships, and the Dutch only twenty-two ships and four fire ships.

John Tyrrell, captain of the *Anne*, rose through the ranks of the navy to lieutenant at nineteen and captain at thirty, and early in 1690 he was appointed the *Anne's* captain. On Monday 30 June 1690 she sailed into battle against the superior French fleet, with a crew of 460, as part of the Anglo-Dutch fleet under the Admiral of the Fleet, Arthur Herbert, Earl of Torrington. The *Anne* was the only English ship to suffer, and it is thought that, despite her heavy armoury, by 2p.m. that afternoon Captain Mees of the *Exeter* sailed between the *Anne* and the enemy in order to give Captain Tyrrell some protection. That night, as fighting continued, the Earl of Torrington ordered the *Swallow* and the *York* to tow *Anne* out of danger. The following morning Tyrrell assessed the damage and reported that over 100 men were killed or wounded, her foremast shot away, and her main mast, mizzen mast and bowsprit in pieces. With his fleet seriously damaged, Lord Torrington ordered a retreat eastwards with the *York* continuing to tow the *Anne*, but the wind rose and became so dangerous that it was decided to run her ashore at Pett Level, between Fairlight and Winchelsea Castle. After beaching at high tide, the crew waited until the evening low tide before coming ashore. That evening Tyrrell wrote to the Admiralty, 'I lie within pistol shot, at high water, of the shore, and at low water, one may walk around the ship. If the French ships do not come in and burn me I hope to save her, though the water comes into her as the tide ebbs and flows.' On Saturday 5 July, the French attacked Hastings and Rye, and that afternoon Tyrrell reluctantly decided to burn the *Anne* so that she could not be taken as a prize. Ironically, soon after this, although they were winning the battle, the French sailed back to France. The consequence of this was Tourville was dismissed for destroying the English fleet, and Lord Torrington court-martialled for cowardice, and imprisoned in the Tower of London to await trail. The burnt-out remains of the *Anne* faded from memory, although the people of Fairlight never forgot her name and tales were handed down from generation to generation. However, in 1974 treasure-hunters took a mechanical excavator out to the ship at low tide and dug into her remains. To prevent further vandalism, that day she became a protected historical monument, and ten years later the Ministry of Defence transferred ownership to the Nautical Museum Trust, part of the Shipwreck Heritage Centre at Hastings, where the fascinating story of the *Anne* is told in detail with many artefacts recovered from the ship on display.

On 19 November 1706 HMS *Hazardous* ran aground in a south-westerly storm near Bracklesham Bay, now another protected site. *Hazardous*, or to give her the French name *Hazardeux*, served in both the French and English navies and was built of oak and pine in Port Louis in 1698, carved and gilded in tribute to the 'Sun King' Louis XIV. Capable of carrying a crew of 350 she was loaned by the French Royal Navy to ship owner and privateer De Beaubriand of St Malo, and by November 1703 was under the command of Captain de la Rue, who dared to venture into the English Channel where she was spotted by three ships of the Channel Squadron under the command of Admiral Sir Shovell. Apparently she put up a good fight against HMS *Oxford*, HMS *Warspite* and HMS *Lichfield*, but despite Captain de la Rue's efforts the official report of the engagement stated that 'she resisted in the most determined way for six hours [and] struck her colours only after she had been reduced to a perfect wreck.' She was towed into Portsmouth harbour as a prize and rebuilt and fitted for the Royal Navy in six months and kept the name, albeit the English spelling. With fifty-four guns, she was

Personal items found on the *Anne* in 1974: a spoon, bottle caps, a buckle and a coin of King James II. (Conrad Hughes, by kind permission of the Shipwreck Heritage Centre, Hastings)

commissioned into Queen Anne's navy on 27 March 1704 as a fourth-rate ship of the line with a reduced crew of 320. For the next two years she escorted convoys across the Atlantic from the New World until November 1706 when she ran into a storm affecting shipping along the South Coast and failed to keep a convoy together. To make matters worse her commander, Captain Brown, was found dead in his bunk, so the vessel came under the command of Lieutenant John Hare who in turn was commanded by Captain John Lowen from a smaller ship, HMS *Advice*. In dreadful conditions Lowen ordered both vessels to come in at St Helen's Road off the Isle of Wight and drop anchor, but in a ferocious south-westerly gale it proved difficult and HMS *Hazardous* ran aground at Bracklesham Bay. Through the crunching of the hull and howling winds, Hare ordered his men to cast cannon and ammunition overboard to lighten the load, but it was too late, the ship became stranded on the beach, close to the Witterings. In desperation Hare requested lighters and men from Portsmouth, but they had to admit defeat, so the order was given to abandon ship. When the storm subsided efforts were made to salvage what they could, but all salvage operations had to be abandoned when waves crashed over the wooden hull. Over the years divers have recovered lead musket balls, pistol shot, a cooking pot and a silver shilling of William III dated 1697. A collection of artefacts tells the story of HMS *Hazardous* at Earnley's Butterflies, Birds and Beasts near Chichester.

The residents of Seaford became known as 'cormorants' or 'shags' a reference to the bird that scours the cliffs and shores seeking out its prey among the smaller species and fish, because they were so efficient in looting the many ships that were wrecked in the bay. One of the earliest to be documented is the *St Paul* sailing from London to Virginia with around £20,000-worth of cargo on board. The story begins on 21 May 1747 when the familiar cry went out, 'There's a ship ashore!' which brought the locals rushing to plunder what they could. In those days French privateers harassed English trading ships, and as the *St Paul* came in sight of Cuckmere, a French clipper lay in wait anchored in the bay ready to pounce. Realising what was happening, the Seaford Customs boat and several local fishing boats attempted to tow the *St Paul* into the safety of the haven to prevent her capture, but the wind and the tide were against them, and she ran aground, on a sandbank. Captain Ragg and his crew were taken off by one of the towing vessels and, as it would be impossible to sail her off the sandbank, it was decided to leave the ship to the French looters. Twenty-three French seamen swarmed onto the *St Paul* and tried to refloat her, but came under a bombardment of musket fire from the Seaford men attacking from the shore, whilst others brought cannon from the fort, dragging it from Seaford Head to Cuckmere, and opened fire onto the deck of the stricken ship. The French privateer soon made off, leaving the prize crew on board the *St Paul* to be taken prisoner. By now, the crew had broken into the ship's liquor store and were too drunk to put up much resistance. It is reported that one of the men who assisted in the event was a Findon blacksmith, William Lassiter, but why he was in the vicinity, some 30 miles from home, is not known, but we do know that he was entitled to a share of the reward money. It appears that the Seaford men involved in the

Cuckmere Haven, showing the Seven Sisters and the coastguard cottages in the 1950s. (By kind permission of Seaford Museum and Heritage Society)

recapture of the *St Paul* quarrelled amongst themselves and the case went to litigation as they could not agree the division of the £1,000 compensation. A notice was placed in the porches of the nearby churches asking for anyone who thought he might have a claim to a share of the £1,000 to go to The Tree public house on 10 March 1748. More than eighty men turned up and each man was rewarded with between £7 and £10. It is claimed that William Lassiter was awarded £7 18s 0d – a vast sum in those days. After everyone had been paid there remained £364 and this was divided between the magistrate and the Customs Officer as their reward for supplying the arms and ammunition for stopping others from looting the ship. The ship was later refloated and able to continue her voyage.

The Seven Sisters cliffs have been witness to the demise of many ships and seafarers, with the local inhabitants quick to arrive on the scene to rescue crews and salvage any valuables for their own gain. There have been numerous casualties between Birling Gap and Cuckmere Haven but wreckers here were not like those in Cornwall and Wales as they did not need false lights to lure the ships on the rocks; location and nature, through the force of the sea, did the work for them.

Probably the greatest and richest shipwreck of all time occurred in 1747, when the Spanish cedar-built ship *Nympha Americana* was captured off Cadiz by Commander George Walker, captain of *The Royal Family* privateer ship. Apparently she put up a good fight before Walker brought his prize through the Bay of Biscay and put into Portsmouth en route to London. The *Nympha Americana* had been on her way to Vera

A 1748 engraving of the *Nympha Americana* by Sussex artist Barrodell Lambert showing the looters around the wreck. (By kind permission of Seaford Museum and Heritage Society)

Cruz with an extremely rich cargo of gold and silver lace, superfine velvets, bales of silks and cloth and £5,000 in cash, as well as £30,000 worth of mercury (quicksilver) used in the refining process. She was on the final part of her journey, under convoy from Portsmouth when she was caught in a storm on 29 November 1747 whilst trying to reach the shelter of the cliffs at Beachy Head. The situation was not good: her crew of 100 were exhausted after a day of struggling with the elements, and waited below deck hoping to beach safely. When the ship hit the rocks, the uppermost section of the hull broke off like matchwood and thirty sailors were thrown overboard and lost. Others desperately tried to save themselves, clinging onto whatever remained of the ship or jumping overboard to swim ashore, including the ship's surgeon who was drowned. The ship finally wrecked at 11p.m. that night, and no doubt all those still on board were praying the old seaman's prayer, 'Oh, God, protect us from the Seaford shags'. The lower portion of the hull had been completely ripped away and was not located until the bitterly cold Christmas Eve.

On the snow-covered beach many Seaford 'shags' and others from surrounding villages gathered like vultures to pick off the best of the spoils. With little compassion they set to work stripping the corpses of any necklaces and ripping open pockets to look for valuables. By now all kinds of booty was being washed ashore, loaded on the backs of horses and carried off at great speed. At some point the vessel's store of liquor was breached and huge casks of brandy came floating ashore. Some looters stacked the casks neatly to be carried away, whilst others decided to open them on the beach, and according to the *Sussex Weekly Advertiser* at the time many were so intoxicated that around sixty people perished in the snow. Records show that a woman was found dead on the beach with her two children weeping at her side. It is not known if she was on board ship or had come to the beach hoping to pick up something to supplement a meagre income, who knows? The Comptroller of Customs, Mr Hurdis, and a few others tried in vain to control the crowd, so Mr Bouchier, Member of Parliament for Southwick, went down with a warrant from the Secretary of War, ordering soldiers stationed along the coast to assist him. The *Gentleman's Magazine* records, 'He met about 12 smugglers with their loading which they abandoned at the sight of the soldiers, but returned the next day in great numbers to retake it, on which, the soldiers firing, killed two and dispersed the rest.'

Thomas Harben, a Lewes watchmaker, bought up large quantities of the quicksilver at base metal prices, which enabled him to buy a fine house in Wellingham, near Ringmer which he dismantled brick by brick, transported and rebuilt at Seaford, known as Corsica Hall and overlooking the sea. Once at Seaford, Mr Harben settled down, resided in grand style, and became involved in much of the town's work.

In 1749, a couple of years later, the Dutch ship *Amsterdam* went down at Bulverhythe and the Mayor of Hastings at the time, William Thorpe, commented, 'This happening so soon after the *Nympha Americiana* has destroyed the morals and honesty of too many of our countrymen for the very people hired to save did little but steal.'

The *Amsterdam's* story begins in Amsterdam in 1748 when she was built for the East India Company and resembled a warship with fifty-four guns mounted on two

1840s engraving of the *Nympha Americana* by J.H. Hurdis. The figure on horseback in the centre of the image represents Mr J. Hurdis, Comptroller of Customs, who was the grandfather of the artist. (By kind permission of Seaford Museum and Heritage Society)

The wreck of the *Amsterdam* at Bulverhythe can only be seen at very low tide. (By kind permission of the Shipwreck Heritage Centre, Hastings)

Deadeye recovered from the *Amsterdam*. These were made of wood encircled with rope or an iron band and pierced with between one and three holes. Three-holed deadeyes are used in pairs, and were used to link ropes to steady the masts. (Conrad Hughes, by kind permission of the Shipwreck Heritage Centre, Hastings)

Uniform buckles recovered from the *Amsterdam*. (Conrad Hughes, by kind permission of the Shipwreck Heritage Centre, Hastings)

gun decks plus a quarter deck. Her captain, Willem Klump, was thirty-three, and lived with his wife and young son in a house overlooking the Prinsengracht in the city. Her maiden voyage was to Batavia, but Willem was very experienced and fully aware of the dangers that a nine-month voyage to the East Indies could bring. On board was a cargo of textiles, wine, stone ballast, cannon, paper, pens, pipes, domestic goods and twenty-seven chests of silver guilder, worth several million pounds in today's money, that was to be sold in China, Japan and Indonesia. On her return voyage she would bring a precious load of silks, spices and porcelain destined for the European market. That November a crew of 203, with 125 soldiers, one male and two women passengers, boarded the ship at Texel but, because of high winds, there were a number of false starts and the *Amsterdam* finally left on 8 January 1749. As she entered the English Channel she encountered a strong gale at Pevensey, and actually struck the seabed, tearing her rudder. Captain Klump sailed on regardless, but his crew wanted to leave the ship immediately and decided to stage a mutiny. The reason for this was not the gale, but during the two-week voyage fifty of the crew members had died, and forty were sick and dying of an unknown disease. Apparently the crew wanted to steer the ship onto the shoreline, but the captain wished to sail on to Portsmouth as soon as the gale subsided. A confrontation ensured that resulted in the crew taking charge of the ship. Chaos reigned and the crew broke into the cargo of wine. Finally she ran ashore on Sunday afternoon, 26 January, and became grounded in the mud at Bulverhythe Bay.

Meanwhile a crowd of spectators and looters had gathered, increasing to over 1,000 by the following morning, and used poles to hook items off the ship, whilst a group of villagers from Hooe, in Bexhill, grabbed bales of velvet and fine cloth off the ship. The crew were brought off the ship, and forty sick Dutchmen lowered over the side and given medical help, and after being looked after locally were returned to the Netherlands. The Mayor of Hastings placed a guard of soldiers around the ship and silver coinage was removed and placed in local authority care. Soon the soldiers and even the salvage workers began stealing as well as the Hastings inhabitants. There were reports also of pilfering from the homes in which the soldiers were billeted but by mid-March salvage efforts were called off and Captain Klump returned to the Netherlands, exonerated of blame, and the file on the *Amsterdam* closed.

As for the *Amsterdam*, she remained waterlogged and sunk into the mud. In 1969 she was discovered after being exposed by a low spring tide with several decks and much of the bowsprit remaining in an excellent condition. She is the best preserved VOC (Verenigde Oostindische Compagnie, founded in the Netherlands in 1602, its purpose to send ships to East Asia to buy pepper, cinnamon and other spices and trade them on European markets) ship ever found, with much of her cargo still on board. The archaeologist Dr Peter Marsden carried out the first survey of the wreck and advised on further excavation, when bottles full of wine, bronze guns and a large variety of objects were found, leading to an archaeological and historical study. The site was designated a protected site under the Protection of Wrecks Act on 5 February 1974 and diving on to or recovering any artefacts is now forbidden. In 1975 a 'Save the *Amsterdam* Foundation' was established in the Netherlands and, using a Dutch-British team of divers and archaeologists, they uncovered part of the lower gun deck, and it would appear that because of the mutiny the ship had been left in chaos as books, food remains, medical equipment and clothing were strewn across the gun deck.

Interestingly some of the artefacts can be linked to their owners. For example, two sisters who survived the shipwreck were Pieternella and Catharina Schook who left aboard a fine dress, part of the quilted petticoat decorated with heart and flowers. Other items found belonging to the sisters were fans, high-heeled shoes and a spoon with the initials PBS – Pietermella Bockom Schook. Captain Klump left behind his sea-chest inscribed with the initials WK, and the skeleton of a dog is thought to have been his. Eventually the Dutch plan to raise the *Amsterdam* and take her back to her birthplace, but for now her remains protrude out of the sand at low spring tides. The story of the *Amsterdam* is told in some detail at the Shipwreck and Heritage Centre at Hastings, along with a collection of some of the finds.

Almost forty years to the day, we hear of yet another wreck in the Beachy Head area. This time it was the *Syren*, a West Indiaman, fifteen weeks into her journey from St Ann's, Jamaica, with a cargo of rum, sugar and pimento. She was driven onto the rocks on Friday morning, 23 January 1789, after running into a violent storm and became a total wreck, her cargo lost. The crew were saved but it appears that only three were fit

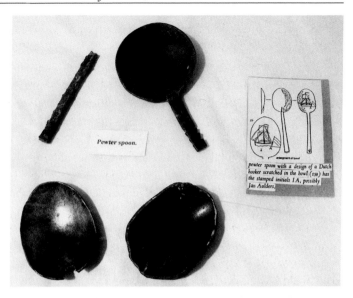

Pewter spoons from the wrecked *Amsterdam* found in 1969. Etched into the bowl is a sailing vessel and the owners initials J.A. – probably a young seaman by the name of Jan Aalders from Amsterdam. (Conrad Hughes, by kind permission of the Shipwreck Heritage Centre, Hastings)

Pewter spoon.

pewter spoon with a design of a Dutch hooker scratched in the bowl (159) has the stamped initials I A, possibly Jan Aalders.

Clay pipes from Gouda, part of the main cargo of the *Amsterdam*. (Conrad Hughes, by kind permission of the Shipwreck Heritage Centre, Hastings)

Clay pipes from Gouda – part of the main cargo. They were packed in boxes surrounded by Buck Wheat.

Wine bottles recovered from the *Amsterdam*. (Conrad Hughes, by kind permission of the Shipwreck Heritage Centre, Hastings)

for work because during the voyage provisions ran short and the crew were rationed to one biscuit a day for two weeks, with only 20 gallons of fresh water between them.

Early parish registers document those drowned men who were given a Christian burial and one such entry in December 1797 informs us that six sailors from the Prussian ship *Ptolemanus* were buried. With a cargo of salt and coffee, it left Liverpool bound for Danzig and during a violent storm struck the rocks off Cuckmere around 10a.m. The sea washed over her but after a series of violent jolts she was pushed further into the rocks and, as so often before, the locals had gathered but there was little they could do except watch the horrors unfold before their eyes. Knowing the ship was likely to go down, the crew on *Ptolemanus* launched a small boat, but it sank immediately with three aboard. One was drowned, but the other two were recovered from the sea. Undeterred, the crew then launched a long boat, but that also filled with water and came adrift. The main mast was cut away, but soon after the vessel broke up. Six perished, but the captain and nine of the crew clung to different parts of the wreck and all but one, a seaman who was jammed between the hull and the anchor, were finally washed ashore at 4p.m. and saved. The trapped man hung on to life, supporting himself on a cable for a further three hours until Mr Langridge of Seaford, Mr Chapman of Eastbourne and several of the Worcestershire Militia stationed nearby went to his aid on a raft. After several attempts they finally reached him, but he had broken his thigh and badly lacerated his legs. He was floated ashore on a plank, and carried by the soldiers to Seaford where he was attended to by a surgeon, but the rescue had come too late and he died the next morning. His body, together with four others, was buried at Seaford churchyard. It was later reported that those who had escaped from the wreck had had some of their clothing stolen!

Seven years later a Swedish galliot, *Ann Amelia*, on her way from Bordeaux to Lübeck with a cargo of wine, foundered off Birling Gap on 16 May 1796. Again the crew were saved but the ship wrecked and the captain, Gottfried Vocking, was not able to prevent the looting of his cargo. Two days after the ship was wrecked, soldiers from the Eastbourne Barracks were called to help unload the cargo, but unfortunately they acquired a taste for the wine that ran from the seams of the ship. They caught the wine in their caps or shoes, and as they became the worse for wear, causing trouble on the beach, the sergeant's guard arrived, ordered them to stop and return to the barracks to be suitably punished.

Two

HMS *BRAZEN*
Newhaven's Biggest Disaster

NEWHAVEN IS no stranger to disasters, but one of the saddest in the town's maritime history must be the loss of HMS *Brazen*, driven on to Ave rocks, a little more than a quarter of a mile from the shore on 26 January 1800, with the loss of 105 lives and only one survivor. The captain was Commander James Hanson R.N., an experienced young officer who had sailed with Edward Vancouver to the Americas and Hanson Point, the southern point of Gray's harbour on the Washington coast. It was so named by Joseph Whidbey, navigator on Vancouver's expedition to the north-west coast of America, but the name did not survive, and it is now known as Point Chehalis. However Hanson Island in Queen Charlotte Sound, north of Vancouver, was named after him in 1860 and still retains the name. It seems so tragic that his brilliant career should have been cut short so abruptly on these treacherous rocks.

At the time of the sinking it was a difficult time for England, at war with France and privateers from both countries scouring the seas looking for ships to capture. In fact HMS *Brazen* herself started life as a French privateer of twenty guns and 170 men named *La Invincible General Bonaparte* and had been operating in the Channel when she was captured on 9 December 1798 by HMS *Boadicea*, a thirty-eight-gun frigate commanded by Captain Richard Keats, who is reputed to have been the first seaman in the navy and was the brother of poet John Keats. *La Invincible General Bonaparte* was just sixteen days into her voyage to Bordeaux. The Admiralty eventually decided to purchase her and she was taken into service on 19 February 1799, and sent to Morwellham Quay on the River Tamar for refitting as a sloop-of-war with sixteen 24-pounder carronades and two 6-pounder guns and renamed HMS *Brazen*.

On 16 January 1800 HMS *Brazen* left Portsmouth with a crew of 120 to sail between the naval base at St Helen's on the Isle of Wight and Beachy Head to 'protect trade and

Hanson Point, now Point Chehalis, at Gray's harbour in Washington State, USA, photographed in July 1980. (Jones Photo Company, by kind permission of Newhaven Maritime Museum)

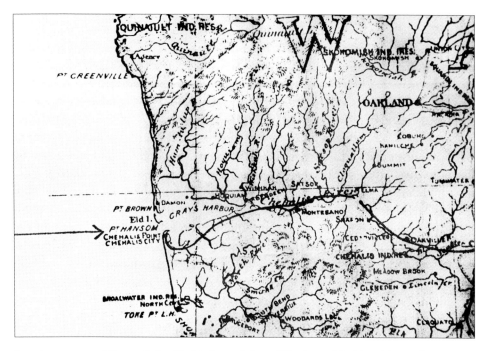

Location on map of Hanson Point. (By kind permission of Newhaven Maritime Museum)

annoy the enemy'. Only the day before she had met a small French ship off the Isle of Wight, which had turned on its heels, but the *Brazen* used all possible sails and soon caught up and took it without a struggle. Captain Hanson was particularly pleased with himself, because the capture had been swift, and he placed his first mate, a midshipman, eight ordinary seaman and two marines on board as the prize crew, who then sailed her to Portsmouth, no doubt looking forward to a share of the prize money. This action ultimately saved the lives of those sailors aboard the prize ship, but may have left the *Brazen* undermanned to deal with the gale it was sailing into.

The story begins to unfold on the evening of 25 January when HMS *Brazen* was travelling eastwards and the wind blew up from the south-west followed by heavy squally rain. Throughout the night the gale increased but the ship managed to clear Selsey Bill; however by 6a.m. the following morning word was received that a large ship, perhaps a man-of-war, was on the shore under the cliffs at Newhaven.

Day had not yet dawned, but an express message was immediately sent to Captain Andrew Sproule R.N. at Brighton who was in command of this part of the coastal defences. Local fishermen, sailors, dock workers and others rushed to the shore where they could hear the mariners' pitiful screams for help, but the flood tide came in so fast that there was little they could do to help. Two lifting cranes, built and stored at the valley behind the cliff top, were brought to the top of the cliff with the aid of eight oxen and men, in readiness to save lives once the tide had receded. These were large cranes with long jibs from which a basket capable of holding three people could be lowered down the cliff face to the beach below. By now the *Brazen*'s main and mizzen masts had fallen overboard, but the spectators could see mariners desperately hanging on to parts that protruded from the sea. Two men jumped into the lifting cage and were slowly let down the 300ft cliff to rescue those floating on the waves. One man drifted towards them, but as they came to his assistance, part of a loose sail was thrown over him and he disappeared beneath the sea. However they noticed another man lashed to a gun-slide being washed ashore under the cliffs and grabbed him and, using a life-saving crane provided by the Royal Humane Society specifically for this purpose, they managed to rescue what turned out to be the only survivor of the HMS *Brazen* and hoisted him to safety. Sadly no further rescue attempts could be made as the sea was now 50ft up the cliffs, and would have endangered the lives of the rescuers. Above the howling wind the rescuers could hear cries from two or three men, and one was seen lashed to the stump of the foremast, but as each wave came in it washed over him until finally he disappeared from view and was never seen again. It was not until 3p.m. that the ebbing tide permitted Captain Sproule's men to get under the cliffs, opposite the *Brazen*, but all they could see was the wrecked ship covering the shore, with bodies strewn along the beach from the wreck to the harbour. Wagons came from Newhaven and took the bodies away, and together with the Collector of Customs from Newhaven and Captain Sproule's men, they gathered up the cannons and any stores that had come

HMS *Brazen* on convoy duty off Selsey, painted by Ted Shipsey. (Conrad Hughes, by kind permission of Newhaven Maritime Museum)

ashore. A few days later the wreck itself broke up and was washed out to sea and disappeared forever.

By February, the sole survivor, Jeremiah Hill, was fit enough to tell his tale. He recalled that he came on watch at 10p.m. on the Sunday night, and during his watch the wind blew up to full scale from the south-west and showed no sign of abating. He was relieved at 2a.m., but due to the conditions he did not go down to his hammock until 4a.m. He was so exhausted that he did not even have the energy to remove his boots. At 5a.m. in the morning, a terrific crash roused him from his half-sleep as the *Brazen* struck the rocks. He raced up on deck with his jacket and trousers still in his hand to find the ship sinking and waves breaking over the deck. He had no time to put either garment on and within moments he was part of a team under John Teague, the ship's carpenter, cutting through the weather shrouds to let the main and mizzen masts go. Captain Hanson gave the order to abandon ship, and he and the purser, Mr Braugh, threw themselves into the water and were never seen again. Together with thirteen or so mariners Jeremiah Hill lagged behind, unsure what to do next as he could not swim, then suddenly the mast crashed onto the decks and the ship was pushed onto her side, with huge waves crashing over her. This sudden topple is the reason no distress signal guns were fired. Jeremiah found the stump of the foremast and clung on desperately as the sky lightened a little and the dark shape of the shore came into view. After about half an hour he noticed a large gun-slide or carriage tethered to a mounting post and threw himself onto the slide and cut it free to allow it to drift into the sea. By the end of February Jeremiah had recovered sufficiently to return to duties, and was paid for his service on HMS *Brazen*.

As late as May of that year, bodies continued to be washed up. Ninety-five bodies were washed ashore in all, and the Admiralty provided rough coffins that were interred at St Michael's churchyard at Newhaven. Ten bodies, including that of Captain Hanson and the purser, were not recovered. Hanson's wife offered a reward for the recovery of the captain's body, which could be identified by an anchor picked out in gunpowder on his arm. The Lords of Admiralty ordered a stone monument be erected, paid for by Captain Hanson's family and designed by architect Mr Henry Rhodes, with inscriptions on four faces. We know the ship was lost in January 1800, but there appears to be some confusion with the exact date as 20 January is etched on the monument, but according to the *Sussex Advertiser* dated 27 January, the event was on 'yesterday morning', making it 26 January. It could be that the monument was erected some months after the disaster and a genuine mistake was made by, for example, difficulty with the handwriting resulting in '26' being confused for '20'. The monument towers over the town of Newhaven and is a fitting reminder of Newhaven's biggest shipping disaster.

Jeremiah Hill being hauled to safety using the crane. (Royal Humane Society, by kind permission of Seaford Museum and Heritage Society)

Face One:

SACRED
To the memory
of
CAPT JAMES HANSON
The officers and Company of His Majesty's ship
BRAZEN:
Who were in a violent storm under the cliff
Bearing from this place S.W.
At 5o'clock Jan 20th A.D. 1800
One of the crew only survived to tell the melancholy tale,
By this fatal event, the country, Alas! was deprived,
Of 105 brave defenders at a time, when it
Most required their assistance;
The remains of many of them were interred near
To this spot,
By the direction
Of the Lords Commissioners of The Admiralty.
'The waters saw thee O God!'

Face Two:

The Brazen, had been ordered to protect this part
Of the coast, from the insolent attacks of the enemy;
And on the evening preceding the sad catastrophy
Had detained a foreign vessel, which was put under
The care of the master's mate, a midshipman,
8 seamen and 2 marines; who were thereby saved from
The fate of their companions.

Face Three:

Names of the Officers lost
James Hanson Esq Commander
James Cook, John Denbry Lieuts.
Archibald Ingram Master
Patrick Venables, James Hanwell Midshipmen
John Braugh Purser Robert Hill Surgeon

Thomas Whitfield Boatswain
Robert Aalder Yawrte Gunner
John Teague Carpenter

Face Four:

The friends of
CAPT HANSON
Caused this monument to be erected
As a mark of their esteem for a deserving officer
and a valuable friend.
It was the will of Heaven to preserve him
During four years voyage of danger and difficulty
In the years 1791, 1792, 1793, 1794
but to take him from us
when most he felt himself
secure.
'The voice of the Lord is upon the Waters.'

Added to the base are the words:

This monument was restored
By Louisa, Widow of the above Capt James Hanson
October 1878

At the time of Captain Hanson's drowning his wife was pregnant, and on 5 May 1800 a son James Hawsey Hanson was born to Louisa at Dartford. On 11 June she brought her five-week-old son to Bexley, Kent, where he was baptised by the Revd William Grem. Sadly on 17 May 1802 the little boy died, just twelve days after his second birthday. When James was drowned Louisa was just twenty years old, she never remarried and lived until 1884, to the grand age of 103, and drew a Naval Officers Widows Pension for eighty-three years, the longest recorded pension in naval history.

In the archives at Newhaven Maritime Museum there is a very interesting poem, believed to have been written at Morwellham Quay, where HMS *Brazen* had been refitted before her fateful journey, but as yet no one has been able to say why it was written:

No Roses Bloom – The Loss of the Brazen

On the night in Morwellham she was married
she was a happy bride
Til the door blew in and the captain
Stood beside her lovers side

Arise, Arise your sailorman
I haste ye along with me
Brazen sails the tide from the convoys side
To chase the French from the sea.

They sailed the tide by the convoys side
Oh they kept the old channel free
Til Brazen drove ashore mid the breakers roar
With the tall Sussex strand on her lea.

Storm and rocks in the night put out their light
And her crew were lost in the sea
And no roses bloom o'er her lover's tomb
For never home came he.

'O' the nights are long
And they have gone,
And the tears have long since dried
Yet we'll ne'r forget those valiant men
And that woeful night that they died.

For when nights are cold
Though we grow old
We shall keep their memory
For no rose bloom o'er a sailors tomb
Beneath yon cold grey sky.

What does this poem mean? Is the bride Louisa or does it refer to the *Brazen*? All we can do until further research has taken place is ponder and surmise.

Captain Hanson was an interesting man, born in Newcastle-upon-Tyne in 1767, and christened at All Saints Church in the town on 26 December 1767. His parents were Hargreaves and Lettice Hanson, *née* Skirrow. His elder brother, John, was a lawyer and remembered as a solicitor, guardian and business agent of George, Lord Byron, the poet. Prior to Lord Byron's birth the midwife, Mrs Mills, who became his nurse, was

A woolwork picture of HMS *Brazen* worked by sailors in the nineteenth century. (By kind permission of Newhaven Maritime Museum)

recommended by Hargreaves Hanson's wife. Byron was born with a caul (the inner membrane originally enclosing the foetus) covering his head. Tradition informs us that a caul is supposed to be a good omen and will prevent the owner from drowning. Seafaring folklore dies hard, and it is claimed that these cauls would change hands for very high prices. James is reputed to have bought the caul from Mrs Mills, but sadly it didn't prevent him from a tragic death at sea so maybe it only works for the person born with the caul. It would seem that as a young boy Byron spent most of his holidays at the Hansons' home in Earl's Court, London, and became very close to the Hanson children. He was at Harrow with one of the sons, and a daughter, Mary Anne, was given away by Byron at her marriage to the Earl of Portsmouth. There are many references to the Hanson family in *Works of Lord Byron, Letters and Journals* (Vol. 1) by Lord Byron and edited by Rowland E. Prothero.

James joined the Royal Navy on HMS *Crocodile* in October 1780 and remained with the *Crocodile* for eighteen months, before joining HMS *Resistance*. Almost two years later he served on HMS *Europa*, but only remained on that ship for three weeks before joining the *Antelope*. He then joined the *Janus* and served for two years before joining the *Porcupine* where he passed his lieutenant's examination. He was selected for the expedition to the north-west coast of America, and on his return became a lieutenant as second-in-command to William Broughton on the *Chatham* which left England on 28 December 1790. When the store ship *Daedalus* arrived in Nootka and Edward Vancouver learned of the death of its commander, Richard Hergest, Hanson was appointed replacement agent (or commander) on 29 August 1972 and promoted up to commander on 24 July 1795. Hanson took the *Daedalus* to New South Wales on two voyages. He then commanded the *Etrusco* and remained with her until he took charge of the sloop *Favourite* in July 1797 and sailed her to the West Indies in January 1798. In November 1799 Hanson was commissioned to HMS *Brazen*, and his appointment is mentioned in a letter from Lord Byron to Hanson's elder brother John:

> Sir,
> ...I congratulate you on Capt Hanson being appointed commander of the Brazen Sloop of War. The manner I knew that Capt Hanson was appointed Commander of the ship before mentioned was this. I saw it in the public paper.'
> I remain your little friend, BYRON

The Sussex song 'The Wreck of the *Brazen*' was composed by a native of Bishopstone in the year 1800, and sung in the Newhaven port area, becoming very popular amongst mariners and fishermen. A copy of the song, given to him by his father, belonged to Mr Walter Eager, one of the watch house staff. It was published in 1911, possibly by the *East Sussex News*, although to date it has been impossible to confirm this:

The Wreck of the Brazen

You seaman all, pray give attention
To these few lines which I am going to tell:
A shocking story I will tell you,
That on the Brazen sloop it fell.

It happened on one Sunday morning,
On January th' twenty-six,
On the high rocks near to Newhaven
The Brazen sloop-of-war did fix.

And when she struck 'twas at low water,
About the turning of the tide;
To tell the power of wind and water
No man was able to describe.

Small bowl, possibly used by
the surgeon Robert Hill on the
HMS *Brazen*. (Conrad Hughes,
by kind permission of the
Newhaven Maritime Museum)

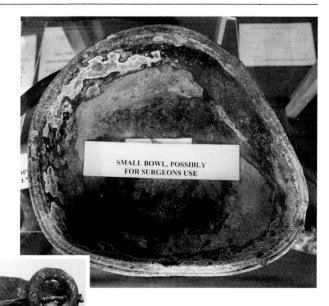

Cooking pot recovered from the *Brazen*.
(Conrad Hughes, by kind permission of
Newhaven Maritime Museum)

Musket balls and cannon flints
recovered from the HMS
Brazen. (Conrad Hughes, by
kind permission of Newhaven
Maritime Museum)

How shocking 'twas to hear the screaming,
The crew so loud for help did cry;
Her masts and rigging were torn to pieces,
Like chaff before the wind did fly.

How shocking 'twas to behold them
That morning when they came on shore:
Pieces of timber, likewise dead bodies
From the Brazen sloop the water bore.

Soon their boats were broke to pieces,
Their precious lives they tried to save;
'Twas all in vain, it proved so fatal,
They sank into a watery grave.

Out of a hundred and sixteen seamen
Only one poor soul got safe to shore;
So shocking was the wreck of the Brazen,
The like was never seen before.

Captain Hanson and his lieutenant
Both stripped and tried to swim ashore,
But sad to say they were exhausted –
Drowned they were and could swim no more.

Captain Hanson has left a widow,
All in distress for to weep;
Like many more on board with him
They all were perished in the deep.

Some had watches, some had money,
Gold rings around their fingers, too;
Some had wives and some had sweethearts –
In sorrow did lament its true.

Now to conclude and finish my ditty;
A mournful tale throughout my song.
May God protect all British seamen
That on the raging seas belong.

Uniform buckles from HMS *Brazen*. (Conrad Hughes, by kind permission of Newhaven Maritime Museum)

Uniform buttons from HMS *Brazen* on display at Newhaven Museum. (Conrad Hughes, by kind permission of Newhaven Maritime Museum)

How shocking 'twas to behold them –
The force of gale it did increase;
There were many on the cliff stood gazing,
But they could render no relief.

May the bright angels rule the ocean
And safely seamen for to guide!
Not like the Brazen that was condemned
Upon Newhaven rocks to ride.

It was through this sinking that a committee was set up in Newhaven to investigate the possibility of establishing a lifeboat station at the harbour and in 1802 Lloyd's was approached for assistance towards the cost. They awarded the committee £50 with the balance being raised locally. A 22ft six-oared lifeboat was ordered from Henry Greathead, whose boats usually cost around £130, and was delivered to Newhaven and entered service in May 1803.

Every year on the anniversary of the sinking of HMS *Brazen* a memorial service is held at St Michael's Church, standards paraded, and wreaths laid in honour of the crew. A lone bugler sounds the Last Post and Reveille.

Memorial in St Michael's Church to
HMS *Brazen*. (Conrad Hughes)

SACRED
TO THE MEMORY
OF
CAPT. JAMES HANSON
THE
OFFICERS AND COMPANY
OF HIS MAJESTY'S SHIP
BRAZEN
WHO WERE WRECKED
IN A VIOLENT STORM
UNDER THE CLIFF
BEARING FROM THIS PLACE S.W.
AT 5 O'CLOCK A.M. JAN. 20TH A.D. 1800
ONE OF THE CREW ONLY SURVIVING
TO TELL THE MELANCHOLY TALE
BY THIS FATAL EVENT
THE COUNTRY ALAS! WAS DEPRIVED
OF 105 BRAVE DEFENDERS
AT A TIME WHEN IT
MOST REQUIRED THEIR ASSISTANCE
THE REMAINS OF MANY OF THEM
WERE INTERRED NEAR TO THIS SPOT
BY THE DIRECTION OF
THE LORDS COMMISSIONERS OF
THE ADMIRALTY

The four faces of the memorial to
HMS *Brazen*. (Conrad Hughes)

THE BRAZEN,
HAD BEEN ORDERED
TO PROTECT
THIS PART OF THE COAST,
FROM THE INSOLENT ATTACKS
OF THE ENEMY,
AND ON THE EVENING
PRECEEDING
THE
SAD CATASTROPHE,
HAD DETAINED A FOREIGN VESSEL
WHICH
WAS PUT UNDER THE CARE OF
THE MASTER'S MATE,
A MIDSHIPMAN,
8 SEAMEN, AND 2 MARINE
WHO WERE THEREBY SAV
FROM THE FATE OF THEI
COMPANIONS.

NAMES OF
THE OFFICERS LOST,
JAMES HANSON ESQ.
COMMANDER
JAMES COOK
JOHN DENBRY } LIEUTS
PATRICK VENABLES
JAMES HANWELL } MIDSHIPMEN
JOHN BRAUGH PURSER
ROBERT HILL SURGEON
THOMAS WHITFIELD BOATSWAIN
....

THE FRIENDS OF
CAPT. HANSON
CAUSED THIS MONUMENT
TO BE ERECTED
AS A MARK OF THEIR ESTEEM
FOR A DESERVING OFFICER
AND A VALUABLE FRIEND,
IT WAS THE WILL OF HEAVEN
TO PRESERVE HIM
DURING FOUR YEARS VOYAGE
OF DANGER AND DIFFICULTY
ROUND THE WORLD,
ON DISCOVERIES
WITH CAPT. VANCOUVER
IN THE YEARS 1791 1792 1793 ...
..... TO TAKE HIM FRO
WHEN MOST HE THOUGHT HIMSELF
SECURE

Three

MULTIPLE SHIPWRECKS
IN ONE DAY

THANKFULLY REPORTS of more than one ship wrecked in a day are few, but when the weather is at its most extreme several ships can become caught up, resulting in the loss of many lives.

The scene that met the residents of Seaford on the morning of 7 December 1809 was one of absolute chaos, and one that many never forgot in their lifetime. The tragedy became known as the 'Seven Ships Disaster' and happened in the days when privateers were authorised by the country's Government to attack and rob enemy vessels during wartime.

Napoleon's fleet had been defeated, but the French were still trying to stifle her enemy by preventing foreign merchant ships from reaching our shores. Ships travelled in convoy and on this particular day the escort ship was the *Harlequin*, leading twenty-two merchant ships through the English Channel as far as Dover. Some of these ships had been captured and re-captured, so the crews on board were well aware of the dangers. The *Harlequin*, armed with twelve 6-pounder and six 12-pounder cannons and a crew of forty-five, was employed to protect the fleet against enemy attack. We could say the *Harlequin* was the shepherd responsible for making sure none of the flock strayed, but in such stormy conditions it was actually the shepherd that led the flock astray when she mistakenly thought the convoy had passed Beachy Head, resulting in the loss of thirty-five seamen.

The tragic story begins on the afternoon of Tuesday 5 December 1809 when HMS *Harlequin*, a hired ship-sloop was escorting a convoy under the command of a young naval officer, Lieutenant Philip Anstruther, from Plymouth for the Downs Roads at the eastern end of the English Channel. Also on board were four passengers, a couple with a two-year-old and a baby. At around 3p.m. that afternoon the signal for sailing was given by the *Harlequin* and the sails on the respective vessels unfurled. The twenty-three ships

Martello Tower No.74, now home to Seaford Museum. It once formed part of the defences built when Napoleon threatened to cross the English Channel in 1803. One hundred and three towers were built from Aldeburgh, Suffolk to Eastbourne. This one was built as an afterthought when it was realised that there was not adequate defence for Newhaven and Tidemills. (Conrad Hughes)

left the port, and a log entry by the captain written on the day of departure shows his frustration with some of the convoy: 'I caused signal guns to be discharged regularly, as handier ships were tending to forge ahead of their allotted station in convoy.' During that night the weather become more turbulent and the shifting winds prevented the more heavily laden ships from making much headway, but slowly the fleet inched its way along the Channel. By Wednesday evening the convoy met a hurricane, the temperatures dropped, and driving sleet and rain made visibility poor, but by the following morning the wind had subsided only to be replaced by thick fog and sleet. The *Harlequin*, as pilot and protector, constantly fired its cannon to alert the convoy of her position, but as the day progressed, the wind and sleet increased and the fog thickened so that by 4p.m. visibility was extremely poor. Lieutenant Anstruther believed the fleet had cleared Beachy Head, and changed course to steer further inshore. In his log he wrote: '(estimate) Beachy Head now due north. Harlequin regains position ahead of convoy. Signal guns fired. Pre-arranged alteration of course to nor'east.' The six leading vessels behind the *Harlequin* – the *Unice, Albion, Weymouth, February, Traveller*

The scene residents of Seaford woke to on 5 December 1809, painted by Ted Shipsey. (By kind permission of Newhaven Maritime Museum)

Engraving of the Seven Ships disaster. (By kind permission of Seaford Museum and Heritage Society)

and the *Midbedacht* – were duty bound to follow their leader, but unfortunately they were not due south of Beachy Head but 3 or 4 miles westwards and sailing towards Seaford Bay. In due course all seven ships ran aground in the bay. The crews had no idea of the danger until they found themselves amongst the violent surf, and all they could hear above the howling wind was the snapping of masts and the ripping of the sails. Huge breakers from the ebbing tide caused the vessels to crash against each other like toy boats to add to the utter confusion. Captain Anstruther's last log entry reads: '5 minutes to morning watch. Wind sou'west abating. Fog. Sleet. Harlequin aground. Signal guns fired and flares to warn convoy. We have serious hull damage reports from below and mid-ships.' Despite the chaos the crew of the *Harlequin* continued to fire cannon warning the rest of the fleet of impending danger due to the navigational error. It was thanks to these efforts that the other sixteen merchantmen of the fleet sailed past Beachy Head without further loss of life.

In an attempt to ease the strain on the *Harlequin*, the crew were ordered to throw all guns overboard and cut away the masts, but two crew members were killed whilst working on deck and washed overboard. We can only surmise what it must have been like for the crew trying to move huge cannons with the ship rocking in rough seas and swell washing over the decks. In such appalling conditions the lifeboats could not be lowered, and the *Harlequin* was the first to strike the shore and astonishingly, no further lives were lost.

Meanwhile at Seaford Head the barge *Weymouth* came crashing through the shallow waters, breaking up beneath the cliffs. Her cargo of tobacco, barilla (a sodium carbonate and sodium sulphate alkali ash produced by burning various Mediterranean plants, used in the manufacture of soap and glass), and cork bobbed among the waves. The *Weymouth* had a crew of ten but only four reached shore. The hero of the rescue was Mr Ginn of Lewes Barrack Department who, at great personal risk, led the rescue and managed to drag the four to safety, including the cabin boy clutching the master's pet raccoon in his arms. He was determined to save the animal as he was so grateful for the kindness shown to him by the master, who on board divided his favours between him and the raccoon. The *Weymouth* knew how dangerous the French privateers could be, and no doubt welcomed an escort, because in the previous month, on 14 November, the ship was captured on her way from Gibraltar in the Channel by a French privateer. The master, John Llewellyn, his wife and the ship's boy were cast adrift in a boat 1km from land and finally made it back to Land's End. However the captors did not hold on to the *Weymouth* for long, a few days later the British man-of-war sloop *Plover* recaptured her under fire from the fort guns at St Malo, and she was taken to the Scilly Isles and reunited with her master. The vessel was then brought to Plymouth where Captain Llewellyn remained to settle matters pertaining to the recapture and put the vessel in charge of his mate.

The *February*, noted for its speed, and in ballast having discharged her cargo at Plymouth, ran aground and dropped anchor, but when the tide returned the anchor prevented the weak, waterlogged vessel from drifting to the shore, and she keeled over.

Her crew of sixteen climbed the rigging until the foremast and the mizzen mast gave way and washed into the sea. They retreated to the main mast, but it gave way under the weight, they too were thrown into the sea, and fourteen were lost. Only the mate, who lacerated his knee, which became inflamed and kept him in bed for weeks, and the ship's boy were saved.

The next vessel to come to grief, half a mile west of Seaford Head, was the small brigantine *Traveller*, which had been driven onto the easterly part of the beach. The *Traveller* was on her way from Malaga with a cargo of dried fruit and sumach, and was another ship grateful for the escort, as she had twice been captured and rescued from French privateers, and not wanting to be taken again, shadowed the *Harlequin* closely. Her entire crew of twelve, including Thomas Coulson her master, were saved by coming ashore before the ship went to pieces, but her cargo was lost.

Not far from the *Traveller* and east of the *Harlequin* the schooner *Albion*, under the command of Captain Jermond, lumbered onto the beach, but the ebbing tide caused her to roll onto her side opposite the Martello Tower, now Seaford Museum. The crew of nine lashed themselves to the rigging calling for help, though in the blinding sleet and wind they were not heard, but eventually all were saved. Part of her cargo of brandy, saffron, cork, wood and almond had been landed at Plymouth Sound but the remainder was still on board.

Just west of the *Harlequin* the American vessel *Unice* ran aground, and Mr Close of Newhaven, together with men from the 81st Regiment, rescued the captain, his crew of ten and a sizeable part of the cargo of cotton, pearl, and potash. Interestingly she was considered to be in excellent condition because only a few months before the fateful day she had £1,000 spent on her.

The *Midbedacht* was another strong vessel, from the same German company as *February*, and was another of the convoy to flounder with such severe force that the main and mizzen masts and her fore-topmast were destroyed when she went aground. Twelve of her crew drowned, only one survived. It was said that the weight of her cargo of brandy, wine, sugar, coffee and other merchandise was responsible for causing her to destruct so quickly. A great deal of the wine was saved, and the local people made good use of the windfall by drinking from anything they could lay their hands on, including hats. Some of the wine-butts floated a considerable distance when the hull broke up, but the Customs officers were eventually successful in securing these for the owners.

It was the firing of the cannons to warn the fleet of pending danger that woke the inhabitants of Seaford that morning, who then flocked to the long stretch of shingle, unable to do much in the thick fog. As streaks of daylight broke through the true horror became apparent. Five ships lay near the *Harlequin* at the east end of the bay and half a mile or so further east was the seventh, the *Weymouth*. The *Sussex Weekly Advertiser* reported, 'They beheld the spectacle that was truly dreadful, the seven ships being high together and complete wrecks, with the remaining crews clinging to differing parts of them, imploring for assistance which is natural in such cases.'

Engraving of the *Harlequin*, 1795–1809. (By kind permission of Seaford Museum and Heritage Society)

Engraving of the *Weymouth*, 1801–1809. (By kind permission of Seaford Museum and Heritage Society)

Engraving of the *February*, 1805–1809. (By kind permission of Seaford Museum and Heritage Society)

Engraving of the *Traveller*, 1776–1809. (By kind permission of Seaford Museum and Heritage Society)

Engraving of the *Unice*, 1804–1809. (By kind permission of Seaford Museum and Heritage Society)

Engraving of the *Midbedacht*, 1795–1809. (By kind permission of Seaford Museum and Heritage Society)

Throughout the morning there were numerous rescues and acts of bravery, and by 10a.m. all that could be saved were ashore, but like all wrecks the local residents were not adverse to a spot of plundering. The *Sussex Weekly Advertiser* at the time reported that it, 'found it hard to record the thieving and looting that went on, being ashamed to mention that such dastardly acts could have been committed at a time of such bravery, sorrow and heroism.' Even before the dark of night had lifted, there were men on the beach drunk to oblivion. Two men who had broached brandy cases died either from exposure due to the foul, freezing weather or from alcohol poisoning.

Even some of the rescuers had their belongings stolen. An officer who had placed his jacket on the beach returned to find his gold watch missing, and Mr Harrison, the Newhaven Customs Collector who helped to save three men, lost his overcoat and boots which he had cast off before rushing into the sea to save a sailor. Whilst some bundled the survivors up the beach to the New Inn (now the Wellington) to be dried, reclothed and fed, others were busy running back and forth between their homes and the beach with the goods they had stolen.

Despite the tragedy that day there was one humorous report. When a rider was hurriedly sent to Blatchington Barracks to inform Captain Browne of the wrecked ships he was caught in a comprising position with Evengeline, the sister of William Catt of Bishopstone Tidemills. Apparently her brother was a pillar of the society, but she was referred to as the 'Tidemills Temptress' and a constant worry to him. Captain Browne was another to fall victim to looters as his greycoat was stolen as he carried out a rescue.

Twelve days later the broken hulls of the ships were auctioned, and on 24 January the insurers auctioned the stores and equipment that had drifted ashore. Bodies from the vessels were washed ashore between 14–21 December and in most of the cases the bodies could not be identified with an individual ship, so the inscription on the graves read 'belonging to one of the above'. Two further bodies were washed up at West Dean and buried there and almost two months later the body of the last seaman to be recovered from the sea was identified as John Callum and buried at Seaford.

The following year a Court of Inquiry was held, and found that no blame should be attached to Lieutenant Anstruther who was allowed to continue his naval career, and rightly so, I feel. He was faced with appalling weather conditions at a time when none of the modern navigation aids were available to him.

In the 1970s a cannon and a bent muzzle with a cannonball still inside was discovered on the seabed at Seaford Bay which probably came from the *Harlequin*, and is now on display at Seaford Museum.

On Saturday 2 June 1860 the morning started with a little light rain and a strong south-east wind which caused the ships on the sea to take refuge wherever they could. By noon the weather improved a little and by 2p.m. it was calm. However it lasted for only around two hours before the wind blew up again, whipping up speed until it was at hurricane level and catching a number of vessels by surprise. It lasted throughout the following day, and left in its wake numerous casualties along the same stretch of shore.

The *Mary* of Portsmouth, a large coal brig, was wrecked west of Worthing, but her crew were saved. The lugger *Lord Nelson* was driven aground east of Worthing and ended up a total wreck, but again her crew were safe, and two other luggers also were driven ashore and completely wrecked. One was the *Eliza* and the other the *Plough* from Whitby laden with stone bound for Arundel, when she was completely wrecked near Shoreham, and her master Mr Peacock narrowly escaped drowning. Two brigs, the *Pike* mastered by George Gallop and the *Richard Foley* mastered by David Hobden, were returning to their home port of Shoreham from Hartlepool laden with coal when they too were caught in the storm. A number of spectators gathered on the shore to watch the ships at anchor, but by 6p.m. the *Pike* was dragging her anchors, one of which broke away from the chains. On inspection the master discovered that the remaining anchor was not capable of holding the ship, and gave orders to slip anchor and make for Shoreham harbour. The anxious crowd looked on as the sea rose and no doubt prayed for her safety, but 100 yards east of the harbour entrance she ran aground, washed by the furious waves. The lifeboat was launched but the surf was too strong to reach the ship, so the coastguards came to the rescue by firing a rocket over the ship and securing a line to enable the crew to pull the lifeboat towards them. Fortunately all the crew were saved, although the ship's boy sustained a broken leg in the rescue. The *Richard Foley* was more fortunate, her anchors held firm until the following morning when she lost both her chains and one of her boats, but later that day she was towed into the harbour. However, later that evening, 2 June 1860, a schooner, the *Mary Ann*, en route from Yarmouth, Isle of Wight, carrying a cargo of coal and under the command of Master Williams, ran ashore on the west side of the harbour. Her sails had been blown away in the storm and she was drifting helplessly, but thanks to a group of people and soldiers stationed at the fort the crew of four were rescued. The master later revealed that he had been shipwrecked on three previous occasions.

Just along the coast, the same storm caused the fishing smack the *William and Eliza* from Brighton to run ashore at Southwick, but her three-man crew and two boys came ashore safely, although in a distressed state. Another victim of the storm was the brig *Transit* en route to her home port of Shoreham with a cargo of coal, when she ran aground to the east of the Chain Pier at Brighton. Within a few minutes she was in pieces, leaving a trail of timber and coal along the beach east and west. Her crew of seven and Captain Grey managed to come ashore. Just opposite the Albion Hotel in Brighton, a French brig, the *Atlantique* of Nantes, carrying a cargo of corn, was forced ashore by the waves taking half the wooden groyne with her. Seven of her crew were saved, but the mate jumped overboard as the vessel struck and was drowned.

Further east along the coast, the storm also was taking its toll, and the *Anne*, a British sailing collier brig on a voyage from Portsmouth to Newcastle-upon-Tyne, in ballast, tried to ride out the storm at Newhaven. She dropped anchor, but around 8p.m. on the Saturday evening she parted company with both her anchors and started to drift towards the beach. She finally came ashore to the east of the harbour entrance and her crew of seven was safely taken off by the Blatchington coastguards under the command of Lieutenant Wollaston R.N., using the rocket apparatus. The last person to leave the vessel was the sixty-two-year-old master, Captain Merrix, totally exhausted, who came safely ashore before the vessel was smashed to pieces by the sea with the wreckage being strewn across the beach. The crew sadly lost all their possessions except what they were wearing at the time. Meanwhile out at sea the *Christel*, a German sailing schooner, capsized off Beachy Head. She was carrying a cargo of wheat from Danzig to Dublin under the command of Master Tschernitz. Fortunately for the crew the *Lively* was nearby and went to the ship's aid, rescuing the crew, and landing them at Deal two days later. A large amount of the debris from the *Christel*, including a chest bearing the name Wihelm Schluter, was later washed up along the beach at Hastings.

Also in the area the *Woodside* was making for the harbour under sail when an enormous wave swept over her just half a mile from safety. The vessel seemed totally lost, but moments later she righted herself and continued to make for the harbour, although she was drifting eastwards and, to those watching on the shore, it was obvious that the crew were not in control. Finally the *Woodside* ran aground around 6.45p.m. with waves continuing to push her further onto the shore. All the crew came safely ashore by knotting a rope around their waists and being pulled through the surf by those on the beach. Unfortunately Master H.G. Dench was lost because he made the error of tying a loose piece of rope to his waist instead of the rope fastened to the vessel, and jumped into the sea expecting to be pulled to safety like the rest of his crew. Edward Mewett, on the shore at the time, saw what happened and dived into the sea, but the master was too far out and eventually disappeared from sight, but another crew member was rescued by boatman Richard Mallett, of Blatchington Coastguard Station. Although the rigging and structure of the *Woodside* were severely damaged the hull was relatively intact, so as the tide receded the cargo of ballast was able to be unloaded.

Another casualty of the storm washed ashore by the weather was the *Margaret*, but this time she came ashore to the east of Newhaven harbour entrance. Fortunately the crew got off the vessel quickly, just before she rolled onto her side and her hull split into two. One half of the hull became embedded in the beach, whilst the other was carried half a mile further eastwards and interestingly, not a single piece of the cargo of coal came ashore.

The next victim of the same storm was the schooner *Eliza Jones*. As she came towards the shore riding on the huge waves, the crew were clinging to the rigging. The mate, Benjamin Thomas, was astride the bowsprit and was saved almost as soon as the ship struck the shore. However it took almost three hours for a line to be set up to reach the others, because the master, James Jones, his crew of two and a boy suffering from exhaustion were on the weather side of the vessel. The uninsured cargo of wheat was washed ashore along the beach.

Next to come ashore was the *Jeune Henri*, a French fishing chasse mare from Dieppe that, like the others that night, was making for the safety of the harbour. Because of the hurricane-force winds, the *Jeune Henri*'s sails were torn to pieces, rendering her unmanageable, so she drifted past the harbour entrance and dropped anchor near to the east pier. Regrettably the anchor was not able to hold the ship in the atrocious conditions and the *Jeune Henri* continued to drift eastwards until she finally ran aground. The vessel was pushed further up the beach with each wave, but all fifteen of the crew were rescued and it was later discovered that very little damage was sustained.

Next to come ashore was the British sailing lugger *John Whiteman*, that was also heading for the safety of Newhaven harbour, but she had lost her sails and became waterlogged as the waves broke over her. In this state Master Clark felt it was safer to run her to shore, and she came to rest close to the others. Suddenly the sea turned her broadside on to the beach, causing little damage but allowing the crew to come ashore safely.

As daylight broke the following morning, Sunday 3 June, spectators at Hastings could see nets and other debris from the fishing lugger *Endeavour*. She had apparently come ashore the previous night around 9p.m., and was now no more than matchwood. Her entire crew, comprising of the owner/master Edward Pomphrey and a crew of six, one of whom had only married on Monday 21 May, were lost.

Daylight also revealed the final casualty of the storm, the *Wonder*, a British sailing schooner from Hastings with a cargo of coal. The ship's timbers were found smashed to pieces over a quarter-mile stretch of the beach, and on close inspection revealed that they were rotten, which may be the reason why the vessel broke up so quickly. Thankfully, unlike the *John Whiteman*, the crew reached the shore safely. A sad footnote to this story is that on Thursday 8 June 1860 two labourers, Richard Simmons and Charles Potter, appeared at Seaford Court charged with stealing from the stricken vessels. They were convicted and sentenced to pay 19s (95p) or one month's imprisonment at Lewes Prison if they defaulted.

Another day to remember was 11 November 1891, when the residents of Worthing woke to a fearsome gale with torrential rain beating down and bouncing off the pavements. Slates were torn from roofs, chimney pots crashed to the ground and the western face for the town clock smashed. It was certainly a day to be indoors, but those who did venture out were blown along the seafront. Around 9.30a.m. the coxswain of the Worthing lifeboat, Charles Lee, could see two vessels drifting close to the shore and fired a maroon to summon his crew. One ship, identified as the German iron barque *Capella* from Hamburg, had left Marseilles in ballast under the command of Captain Martens and a crew of eleven. She had been battling the sea for two days and just as the maroon sounded she struck the beach opposite Heene Terrace.

The second ship, the *Kong Karl* had left Liverpool on 28 October 1891 bound for Christiania with a cargo of coke under the command of Captain Jornson, plus a mate, a crew of four, and a boy. In severe weather she lost her way in the Atlantic and was proceeding up the English Channel when she ran into a gale on 11 November and ended up drifting half a mile from Lancing. Because of the heavy seas it took the lifeboat crew a full sixteen minutes to launch the *Henry Harris*. Once afloat, the coxswain decided he

Kong Karl beached at Worthing. A horse and cart stand by and Worthing Pier can be seen in the background. (By kind permission of the West Sussex County Council Library Service)

could not attend both boats, and took the decision that the wooden schooner *Kong Karl* was in more danger of being smashed to pieces. Launching into high tide the *Henry Harris* filled with water at least six times on her way to the *Kong Karl*.

Meanwhile at West Worthing, with the *Capella* still flying her distress signal, local fisherman Harry Blann, fearing her crew of twelve would be drowned, mustered a crew together and launched a ferry boat. Many within the fishing community helped to drag the boat along to West Worthing and the crew of fourteen fishermen set out in the tempestuous sea, but came ashore three times whilst trying to rescue the crew on the barque. Heavy-hearted, they had to admit defeat and exhausted gave up the struggle.

Meanwhile the *Henry Harris* had more success and managed to reach the *Kong Karl* around 11a.m. and boatman Harry Marshall, Worthing's first official lifeboat bowman, managed to attach a line to the stricken ship, that the crew used to bring the lifeboat alongside and hold her firm to enable the crew of seven to jump onto the lifeboat. With the last man safely aboard the line was severed and the *Henry Harris* could make her way to the shore, landing at Lancing around 11.45a.m. to the cheers of the many spectators who had gathered. The Norwegian crew were taken to Lancing Coastguard Station before being sent to Mr Brown, the Swedish Norwegian Consul at Shoreham harbour.

With the crew of the *Capella* safely ashore, the lifeboat crew, in hurricane-force winds, relaunched the *Henry Harris* and by 2p.m. reached the stricken *Kong Karl*. They found five of the crew had already landed in their own jolly boat, leaving the captain and six of the crew to be rescued by the *Henry Harris*. The *Kong Karl* began to drift eastwards towards Worthing Pier and, fearing problems, the pier directors met with the Lifeboat Chairman, Mr Hargood, and Coxswain Charles Lee and decided that Coxswain Lee should board the ship and drop her anchors.

Early the following morning two tugs came from Shoreham, watched by a crowd of spectators, and saw the *Capella* towed out to sea around 8a.m. Unfortunately they encountered trouble entering Shoreham harbour, so the ship was towed to Newhaven instead. The lifeboat crew – Coxswain Lee, Bowman Harry Marshall, Fred Marshall, George Wingfield, George Belton, Jack Elliot, Fred Wakeford, Peter West, Frank Burden, William Collier, Tom Wingfield, Luke Wells and Steve Wingfield – were each awarded 10s (50p) per rescue, making a total of £1 each for their day's work. The men were also invited to a dinner at the Minor Hall on 16 November where, after the meal, clay pipes and tobacco were distributed to them. On 9 December a photographer, Mr E. Pattison Pett, presented each of the members of the lifeboat crew with a copy of the photograph taken a couple of weeks earlier, and printed in the illustrated weekly magazine *The Gentlewoman*, with the following verse:

A Gallant Lifeboat Crew

Oh! Men of Worthing town,
That in the salt sea sail,
Where the breeze from Findon down
Swells on to meet the gale.

Oh! Men of Worthing town
That fear no sea-born wind,
You smile at Neptune's frown,
And count the storm too kind.

Oh! Men of Worthing town,
To you the well won palm;
Long may ye sail and fear no gale,
To end your days in calm.

At an RNLI committee meeting held in London on 10 December it was decided to present a silver medal and framed vellum inscribed to 'Charles Lee, for his courage in rescuing two crews during that gale in November.'

A tribute to these brave Worthing men was penned by the Revd William Davison, Minister of the Chapel of Ease (St Paul's) in Chapel Street:

The Wreck of the Kong Karl

I was sitting in my vicar's room,
When I heard the Coastguards' dreadful boom,
It was the summons to obey,
And there and then the lifeboat men
Dashed in the leaping, foaming bay.

What a dreadful day it was that day;
The town was filled with a wild dismay –
A wreck, a wreck! Oh can it be?
And with the throng I ran along
Down to the heaving boiling sea.

The sky was dark with an awful frown
And the blinding wind and rain came down,
Mountainous waves came rolling in;
With mighty roar they lashed the shore,
And then died with a fearful din.

Many a brown waving hand was seen
To cheer the hearts of the brave thirteen,
Many a cheering word is thrown
As on they go, breasting the foe,
To save men's lives and risk their own.

Just like a chip the lifeboat is toss'd.
Now on a wave and now as if lost,
The very billows fail to check;
Still on they ride o'er raging tide
On, on to the wreck! To the wreck!

Fiercer and fiercer the tempest grew
Over the heads of the noble crew,
The very heavens seem to rend,
And with a shock, as on a rock,
The Worthing lifeboat stood on end.

The cry goes up. She's lost to sight!
And then a murmur, All is not right!
Good Lord protect the lifeboat crew!
We see the wreck, all hands on deck,
Waiting, praying for the rescue.

She's there! She's there! And their eyes they strain,
And they shout Thanks God, she rides again!
Down on the wreck she, heading fast,
O'er hissing wave still mounts the brave,
Three cheers, she gained the wreck at last!

The crew is safe in the Worthing boat,
And the wreck is left to sink or float:
Back, back they come with full bent oar,
And now a cry reaches the sky–
The shipwrecked crew are safe on shore!

Today the figurehead from the wrecked *Kong Karl* and Coxswain Charles Lee's silver medal can be seen in Worthing Museum, whilst on the promenade near the beach office can be seen a capstan said to be made from a boom (a sailing beam to which the bottom edge of a sail is attached) from the *Kong Karl*.

Sadly in the heat of the moment the crew of the ferry boat who so bravely attempted to rescue the *Capella* were forgotten, and not even invited to the dinner held on 16 November. However the town of Worthing had not forgotten and spoke of their courage, and were keen to give them a donation, particularly as the weather had prevented the fishermen from earning any money to provide for their wives and children. A most respected gentleman of the town wrote:

The attempts made by 14 Worthing watermen and fishermen during the height of the gale on Wednesday morning last, to rescue the crew of the stranded barque off West Worthing seem to call for some slight acknowledgement, and subscription are therefore respectfully invited to form a fund for purpose of giving each of the men a small gratuity for their praiseworthy and plucky endeavours to render assistance.

Contributions came in from His Worship the Mayor and other civic dignitaries as well as from the townsfolk. The fourteen fishermen and water men – Harry Blann, Bill Blann, Mark Marshall, Arthur Marshall, Richard Cusden, Charles Stubbs, William Poland, Jo Street, John Riddles, James Tester, Charles Lambeth, Frank Collier, James Medhurst and Tom Giles – each received 9s 3d from the fund.

A capstan situated near the Beach Office at Worthing, said to be made from a boom from the *Kong Karl*. (Conrad Hughes)

Later on that morning of 11 November 1891 news was received of a beached sailing ship at Portslade and those who rushed to the scene saw the French *Ville de Napoleon* lying on her side, her crew clinging to the rigging. The coastguard officers from Southwick and Hove quickly arrived and made several attempts to fire a line onto the ship against the gale before finally securing a line and hauling all the men to safety by breech buoy.

They had been clinging to the rigging for so long that they were numb with cold, their clothes reduced to rags. Some of the spectators remained on the beach to watch the *Ville de Napoleon* rocking in the stormy sea and after a while someone shouted that another vessel was in trouble. They scoured the sea and could just make out the shape of a two-masted schooner within 100 yards of the water's edge. The *John and Robert* had left North Wales with a cargo of slate and the severe gale had blown all her sails away except for the mainsail, as the waves crashed over her. The mate steered for the *Ville de Napoleon* in the hope that she was heading for safety, but she too ended up on the beach, her crew of four clinging to her rigging. An urgent message was sent requesting the coastguards to return with their rocket apparatus, but they took over an hour to get back. Just after 2.45p.m. the first line was fired, but it missed the target. The second went nearer but it

An example of a breeches buoy used in the rescue of the crew on the *Ville de Napoleon*. A line is connected between the rescuers and the shipwreck, and a seat in the form of a pair of leather shorts is suspended from the line, and pulled along. (By kind permission of Tony Daly)

was third time lucky for the line to fall onto the ship. The ship's mate secured the line, but he was then hit by a huge wave, incapacitating him. During the voyage the crew's provisions had become contaminated, so, weak and hungry, they were unable to haul in the rope of the breeches buoy. Frantically the spectators signalled instructions to them, but as the waves continued to wash over the decks, they retreated to the bowsprit. By now the crowd were calling for the lifeboat, but they didn't know that the gale had deposited mud across the harbour entrance. They could do nothing but wait for the tide to rise. Eventually the lifeboat was launched at 3.30p.m., but despite rowing out three or four times, each time they had to return knowing that crossing the bar of mud would result in the boat capsizing. Around 4p.m. the coastguard asked the harbourmaster for help, but it seemed a hopeless situation. The chief coastguard knew he had to do something so telephoned the Brighton lifeboat for assistance, but could not get through as a clerk at Brighton was using the line. However the clerk heard over a cross line, 'Send the lifeboat', and with another delay obtaining permission, time was fading for the crew on the *John and Robert*. A wave washed a young lad from the bowsprit and within a few minutes his bruised body rolled in on a huge breaker and, despite attempts to revive him, he died. The mate, Thomas Hills, revived a little and told the crew that he was going ashore. Grabbing the rocket line he dropped into the sea, but the breakers were too strong and he was washed ashore, where amazingly he regained consciousness and was taken to the Adur Hotel where he fully recovered. The rest of the crew remained clinging to the bowsprit, and in the fading light the spectators lost sight of them but the captain's body came ashore, just as the Brighton lifeboat arrived. Less than a minute later the ship gave a huge heave and the remaining sailor, a seventeen-year-old clinging to the bowsprit, disappeared into the water and his body was washed ashore the following day. All three from the *John and Robert* were buried at St Leonard's, Aldrington and the tomb can be seen at the rear of the churchyard.

Further along the coast there was no let-up in the weather for the people of Hastings, especially with a force 10 south-westerly gale howling. Out at sea the *J. C. Pfluger* had left San Francisco 145 days earlier bound for Bremen with a general cargo. In command was master, H. Kruse, with a crew of sixteen, together with a male passenger who came aboard at Honolulu and a woman and two young children. Conflicting newspaper reports state these were the wife and children of the passenger or the master. By 5a.m. the wind was at its most vicious and the vessel was being blown off Bexhill with her sail gone, dragging both anchors, and flying the distress flag. Every high wave blew her nearer to the shore, and the coastguards at Pevensey, Kewhurst and Bexhill were alerted and they made for St Leonards, as it was clear that the vessel was likely to come ashore there. The coastguard stations at Hastings and Bo Peep were also alerted and the rocket apparatus made available at Bo Peep, dragged to the beach by a wagon pulled by three horses.

Meanwhile on the *J. C. Pfluger* the crew and passengers gathered at the wheel, every wave washed over the deck with such force that the spray drenched them. Eventually at 9.30a.m., still dragging its anchors, the vessel became stuck in the sand 300 yards from the beach, off West St Leonards railway station.

The rocket apparatus was positioned for firing, but the first attempt fell 50 yards short of the vessel because of the strong winds and it took fourteen rockets before a line was actually attached to the vessel. Half an hour later the Hastings lifeboat, *Charles Arckoll*, arrived and was launched under the command of Coxswain Swaine and Sub-coxswain Moon, but no sooner had she entered the sea then the strong wind pushed her eastward and back towards the shore, despite all oars being double-manned. This caused the *Charles Arckoll* to go beyond the *J. C. Pfluger* and was unable to perform a rescue. Throughout the coastguards continually fired the rocket line until finally Chief Officer Cox took the rocket launching tripod under the shelter of a nearby groyne to protect it from the wind and fortunately the line went right across the vessel onto the rigging on the foremast, where two of the crew secured it. The coastguard positioned the rescue equipment directly opposite the vessel, and instructed the crew to start hauling the line to which ropes and blocks had been fixed. But it didn't go according to plan, because the action of the sea twisted the ropes, which necessitated two of the *J. C. Pfluger* crew sliding down the line to free the block by unwinding the ropes, not an easy task with the weather as it was. After an hour the block was freed allowing the hawser to be pulled ashore by the coastguards and over-eager helpers, who had to be restrained before they did some serious damage. With the hawser finally secure the first person into the breeches buoy was a crew member, August Englebart, because the

J.C. Pfluger ashore at Hastings on 11 November 1891. (By kind permission of Hastings Library and David Renno)

master decided he wanted its safety tested before allowing the female passenger to use it. The first part of the seaman's journey from high up the foremast meant he cleared the rough sea, but on the final leg was actually dragged, exhausted through the sea until close enough to the shore for the rescuers to wade in and save him. One of the spectators realised the problem and erected two scaffold poles as an A-frame to raise the buoy hawser high above the sea on the shore end to enable those rescued to be in the sea for less time. A second man then came ashore carrying one of the children followed by a steady stream of men, but the mother of the children, unable to climb the foremast, had to be hauled up by the crew. The last man, the master, left the vessel at 4p.m. One of the crew sustained a broken leg getting off the vessel, but the rest came ashore safely, and were cared for by the Shipwrecked Mariners' Society, before being taken to rest homes.

Mr Collard, the owner of the steamer *Nelson*, offered to pull *J.C. Pfluger* off the sand but the master refused as he wished to await news from the owners in Germany. Meanwhile the vessel was being pushed further eastwards by the sea and wind, and by the following day had travelled 250 yards further east and it was agreed that four tugs would be paid 1,000 guineas each if successful on the following Tuesday, but nothing if they failed. By now hundreds of spectators arrived on the scene, with every train stopping at West St Leonards station bringing even more, causing disruption to the town.

No sooner had the crew of the *J.C. Pfluger* been rescued than the *Nerissa*, a British sailing schooner with a cargo of slate from Port Madoc bound for Stettin, was seen off St Leonards at around 6.30p.m. flying a distress flag. The *Nerissa*, under the command of Master Jenkins, with a crew of three and one boy, had encountered problems at around 2a.m. whilst off Beachy Head. She had been caught in the horrendous storm and the force of the waves caused her to leak. The crew manned the pumps, but soon discovered they were unworkable, and as the vessel filled with water it became more difficult to sail, and her crew spent the day struggling in dreadful conditions. As the wind drove the vessel through the waves and surf, the crew climbed the rigging to prevent them from being washed overboard. The *Nerissa* ran aground opposite Marine Parade in Hastings at 7p.m. having followed the instructions of those on the shore as the best place to beach. As soon as she came ashore she turned broadside on so that the waves beat at the vessel, tearing the sails and snapping the fore topmast which fell over the side of the vessel. The coastguards, still in wet clothes, were on the beach, having just completed the rescue from the *J.C. Pfluger*. Now they had the problem of getting the line onto the vessel, and this was only achieved when one local man had the courage to wade into the sea and secure a line to the vessel. The crew took it in turns to be hauled to safety by the breeches buoy, and the last to leave, the master, was about to get into the breeches

Nerissa ashore at Hastings on 11 November 1891. (By kind permission of Hastings Library and David Renno)

buoy and jump over the side when a large wave struck the ship and caused the vessel to roll. The master disappeared from view and it was feared that the ship may have rolled onto him but then he was spotted on the top of a wave, and around twenty men rushed into the sea and pulled him, semi-conscious, ashore to be taken into care with his crew by the local Shipwrecked Mariners' Society agent. Later, when the master recovered, he said that he had been a cod fisherman for ten years off Newfoundland, had crossed the Atlantic Ocean twice in the *Nerissa* and had been run down by a man-of-war whilst in the Mediterranean, but the conditions of 11 November were the worst he had ever encountered. As morning broke the following day the *Nerissa* was roughly in the same position and stuck fast into the sand. Luckily there was little damage to her hull, although the deck and bulwarks were severely damaged. The crew set about removing the cargo, but they had not completed the work when the next incoming tide, accompanied by the worsening wind, completely destroyed the *Nerissa* by 7.30p.m. that evening.

Three years later, two ships were caught in another tremendous storm with heavy rain and hail during Saturday 20 and Sunday 21 October 1894. Sitting it out at Seaford Bay was the tug *Irene*, owned by Trinity House, that was towing the Trinity House decommissioned lightship *Warner*, known as Light Vessel No.22. This was one of the floating lights to mark the waterway through the Solent at Spithead and was being taken to London for repairs. Both ships had dropped their anchors as well as the towing hawser and were sitting out the gale when at around 4.30a.m. the storm reached its height, the towing hawser snapped, and put so much strain on the anchor cable it also broke, leaving the lightship drifting towards the shore. The crew of the *Irene* launched their lifeboat in an attempt to get a line onto the lightship but they soon got into difficulties so another small boat was launched from the lightship, but this too got into difficulty. Both boats tried to return to their respective vessels but were driven back by the raging sea. The crew on the drifting lightship were unable to raise a distress signal because all their equipment had been removed and taken on board the lightship that replaced it in the Solent. Luckily the Blatchington coastguard saw the lightship dragging her anchor and arrived on the beach as the two small boats approached. In the first boat were three men but it capsized and smashed to pieces. Two of the coastguards, together with Sergeant Instructor R.E. Davis of 'C' Company Seaford Engineers, dashed into the sea, but only managed to rescue one seaman called Fuggle who was brought to the shore on the verge of death, and it took Instructor Davis twenty minutes to revive him. Sadly the other two men drowned.

The officer in charge of the coastguard station arrived with the rocket apparatus, but by now the lightship had run aground at Seaford. The first two shots failed to reach the ship but on the third attempt a line was secured, and those still on board were able to come ashore. The second small boat with three men aboard capsized, one managed to reach the shore, but the other two drowned.

The following day, Monday 22 October, the body of one of the drowned men, William Stone, aged twenty-eight, was found near Cuckmere and identified by

Benjamin John Taylor, who lived with him in East Cowes, Isle of Wight. An inquest was held at Cuckmere and the jury recorded a verdict of accidental drowning. Later Sergeant Instructor Davis was presented with a gold watch by 'C' Company together with a letter from the Commander-in-Chief, in recognition of his efforts to save the life of Fuggle.

Caught up in the same storm on Sunday 21 October was the British sailing Thames barge *Alice Little* on a voyage from London to Southampton with a cargo of barrels of oil and petroleum. At 6.30a.m. that morning during the storm the master, Thomas Gurr, decided to make for the safety of Newhaven harbour, but she lost her sails in the storm and the anchor was dropped just east of the harbour to ride out the storm. Around this time the officer in charge of the Newhaven Coastguard Station became aware of the vessel's plight and mustered his crew who set off to help, but as soon as they reached the harbour mouth they realised that their boats was useless in such heavy seas, and put ashore on the east side of the harbour, continuing on foot along the beach carrying the rocket apparatus. By 7.15a.m. the *Alice Little* had lost her anchor cable and was driven ashore to the east of the harbour, and the moment the vessel hit the shore huge waves swept along the full length of her putting the lives of the three-man crew in danger. The master could be seen struggling in the water and Timothy McCarthy, one of the coastguards, quickly grabbed a lifebelt and line and ran into the sea to rescue him, and brought him ashore. McCarthy went back into the sea with a colleague, Mr W. Honey, and both swam out to the stricken ship and secured a line. With the aid of the line they soon brought the other members of the crew safely ashore. Over the next few hours, the rough sea dislodged the barrels of oil on deck, so gangs of men were called upon to recover as many as possible as they washed ashore. By noon *Alice Little* began to break up, resulting in the barrels escaping from the hold, and although some smashed open, the majority remained intact, and soon after the vessel was lost to the sea.

Four

INTO THE ELEMENTS THEY WENT
Times of Gales, Fog, Wind and Rain

ONE OF the biggest disasters to hit the seafaring community of Worthing happened on a wild and stormy Monday 25 November 1850 when the ferry boat *Britannia* went to the aid of the *Lalla Rookh*, and capsized with the loss of eleven local fishermen.

As dawn broke the fishermen gathered on the beach in a biting south-westerly wind. The sea was particularly rough, and as these were the days before the lifeboat station had been set up, these 'good Samaritans' scoured the horizon to see if any ship was in distress. One of the fishermen spotted a barque, about 3 miles out, with only two of its three masts intact, flying a distress flag. The *Lalla Rookh*, an East Indian trading vessel, had left Brazil for its home port of London with a cargo of rum and sugar under the command of Captain W.H.P. Hains and a crew of nine. She had got into difficulties so the crew cut away the main mast in order to prevent the barque from keeling over, as with her sails blown away she was in danger of coming ashore. Without thinking about their own lives, the fishermen set out from Worthing beach in a ferry boat that could hold thirty belonging to Sydney Beck, a local innkeeper. There were plenty of willing hands to launch the boat as the fishing community turned out in force, and just after 8a.m. she was afloat. The ferry boat battled through the breakers, hoisting its foresail on the main mast, a mizzen sail from the stern and a topsail from the topmast. Residents swarmed onto the beach to watch, but were forced to retreat when the tide turned and flowed in at an alarming rate. Suddenly they noticed the distress flag on the *Lalla Rookh* being lowered and assumed *Britannia* had reached her. Then silence fell as they realised the signal colours were raised again in great haste as both vessels disappeared from sight. Twenty or more of the Worthing fishermen became so concerned for their colleagues that they decided they could not wait for news and launched a larger two-masted lugger, normally used on longer fishing trips, to search for the stricken ship and the fishermen. They rowed until they saw the *Lalla Rookh* which had dropped anchor, but there was no sign of *Britannia* or the fishermen. Repeated attempts were made to fix a line on the ship until one was secured and the fishermen were hauled towards it. One of the fishermen shouted across the howling wind to the captain, enquiring about the fate of the *Britannia* and her crew. The answer received numbed everyone, as the captain explained how the ferry boat came within 200 yards before being swamped by the sea and capsized. He could see four or five people clinging to the upturned boat then they drifted past and out of sight. Captain Hains was about to send one of their boats to their aid but realised it was too dangerous and knew he risked losing his crew as well. When the lugger arrived, the *Lalla Rookh*'s jolly boat was lowered and nine of the men from the lugger jumped into it in threes, until the captain had enough extra help for him and his crew to rig up fresh sails to the two remaining masts, and the *Lalla Rookh* was left to continue her journey.

The remaining fishermen made their way back in the stormy sea to Worthing, and as they dragged themselves from the boat exhausted, muttered to the anxious onlookers, 'All are lost.' Screams of disbelief echoed along the beach, whilst others were shocked into silence, and the mournful sobs of the widows and fatherless children could be heard above the wind. The Newman family were the worst affected with four members of their family lost: Harry Newman, aged forty-seven left a wife and eight children; his brother Jim, aged fifty-one, the eldest of the crew, left a wife and seven dependent children, and on hearing of his death and the loss of two of her elder sons Mrs Newman was struck dumb and remained so for a while; another son, John, aged twenty-six, was married and his wife had given birth that morning, so news of her husband's death was kept from her until she recovered; his brother, Jim junior, aged twenty-one, the youngest of the crew, was a bachelor. Bill Hoskins, aged thirty-seven, left behind a wife and four children; John Belville, aged forty-nine, a wife and five children; Harry Bacon, aged forty-eight, left a wife and six children; and Bill Wicks and Harry Slaughter, both aged twenty-eight, were bachelors. In his book, *A Town's Pride*, Rob Blann states that his research revealed the doomed ferry *Britannia* was washed ashore, upturned near to Hove Gap that same afternoon, and the body of Steve Edwards, aged forty, was picked up on Hove beach at 7.30a.m. the following morning, He left a wife and four children. During the third week of December the bodies of five of the drowned men were washed ashore between Worthing and Newhaven, and Harry Bacon, Bill Wicks, Jim Edwards, Jim Newman senior and John Belville were buried at Broadwater. Soon after Christmas the eighth body, that of Bill Hoskins, was washed ashore, but the others were never found.

The Revd William Davison, Minister of the Chapel of Ease (St Paul's), Chapel Road, set about researching into the needs of the bereaved families and at a public meeting on Thursday 28 November gave the names of the nine widows and forty-seven fatherless children. There were also three elderly parents partially dependent on men who died. A nationwide appeal for the widows and orphans resulted in over £5,000 being raised. Sadly only two reminders of Worthing's most tragic event are left, a stone tablet in Broadwater Church, and a nineteenth-century poem:

In November, eighteen fifty,
When the winds were fierce and shifty,
And the seas swept with a grinding roar,
On Worthing's stony beach,
Scudding swiftly on before them
Drove the Lalla Rookh for Shoreham,
Barque ill-fated, heavy freighted,
For a port she ne'er would reach!

Broke this morning wild and gusty,
And the boatmen, sage and trusty,
Shook their head and gave you warning
Not to put to sea that day.
'There's some dirty weather brewing,
There'll be ugly business doing!'
'Will that barque fetch up to Shoreham?'
'Shouldn't like, sir, yet, to say.'

'For the wind, sir, looks like shiftin',
And to leeward she'll be driftin',
And – just look, sir – it has caught her
Dead athwart her starboard bow.
No – it warn't, sir, quite judicious.
With the weather looking vicious,
To hug the land so closely –
It's an awkward case, sir, now!'

Darker grew the sky each minute,
And a storm, with fury in it,
From the south-east, hoarsely growling,
Burst upon the labouring ship.
Lightening rent the clouds asunder –
Hoarser, hoarser, growled the thunder,
And the savage, hissing breakers,
Seeded to hold her in a grip.

Nearer, nearer came she landwards –
Ever nearer, nearer, sandwards,
Where the foam and fleck were showing
Where good ship might find a grave
And the surf leaped up around her,

And a rock and sandbank ground her,
And the watchers cried, 'It's over
If we haven't strength to save.'

Then stood forth a good and true man
Of the fisher folk, James Newman,
And he cried, 'I can't stand idle
While those shrieking fellows die.
It's quite possible to save 'em –
Perils are there? Well lets brave 'em.
They're our brother men, mates, aren't they?
Harkye, I, for one, shall try!'

Then his two sons and his brother
Said each, I will, for another, –
And James Edwards and six more at once,
Stood forth and made a crew.
Then they ran a boat out quickly,
Through the rollers, coming thickly,
And the foam dashed from the oar-blades,
Now on high, now lost to view.

On they lifted, fiercely straining,
And the goal were nearly gaining,
When a monster sea burst on them
With a rush and sullen roar.
With a desperate strength they drove her,
But the good boat toppled over,
And of all that brave eleven,
Living soul ne'er reached the shore.

Ye who love our folk seafaring,
And their kind hearts and their daring,
Bend your steps some summer evening
Mid Broadwater's roadside graves,
These on tombstone, plain and hoary,
you can read this simple story
And lament these gallant victims
To the fury of the waves.

Soon after this tragic event the inhabitants of Worthing began another fund subscribing to the town's first lifeboat, a self-righting vessel, which came into service in 1853.

Further east on St Valentine's Day 1882 the steamship *Gannet*, on a voyage from Calcutta via the Suez Canal to London, was coming up the Channel laden with a cargo of tea, coffee, wheat, linseed, cotton, indigo, hides, stags' horns and wood, estimated to be worth £120,000, and ran aground. On board was her Captain W.C. Smith and a crew of thirty-six.

Her problems began on Monday 13 February when she ran into thick fog and a south-westerly force 6 gale, requiring her to sail closer to the shore than usual. Her captain also made the mistake of assuming that the lights at Newhaven were further on ,believing he had actually cleared Beachy Head. The crew did not realise their position until they were east of Newhaven, and immediately put their engines into reverse. Unfortunately it was too late, and the vessel struck the shore broadside on at 2.30a.m. on the morning of Tuesday 14 February, and because of the heavy seas drifted further east, and came to rest between the Assembly Rooms and Martello Tower. The crew fired several distress rockets, and sounded the ship's whistle to attract attention.

Meanwhile, on lookout duty at Blatchington Coastguard Station, George Doran noticed the *Gannet* and informed his officer in charge, who, together with a number of men, set off with the rocket apparatus, knowing it would be impossible to launch the boats. The first rocket fired went over the vessel, securing a line to the *Gannet*; twenty men were hauled to safety by breeches buoy and taken to the Bay Hotel, but the remainder decided to stay on board until low tide.

At 6a.m. Newhaven's lifeboat, the *Michael Henry*, was towed out by the steam tug *Tipper* to offer assistance. This was to be the lifeboat's first active service, but on this occasion it was not required. By 7.30a.m. huge crowds of spectators gathered on the shore waiting for the tide to recede as one of the crew on the *Gannet* jumped over the side of the ship into the sea. One of the coastguards dashed into the sea and managed to haul him to safety, although he was unconscious and remained so for some time. It later transpired that the seaman had been drinking after arguing with a fellow crew member and jumped overboard. By mid-morning the tide had ebbed sufficiently for both crew and spectators to start to unload as much cargo as possible and by the time the tide had returned they had salvaged 120 tons. However, the incoming tide was accompanied by high winds and thick fog and, despite the help of four powerful tugs, all hope of refloating the *Gannet* was abandoned. No doubt because of the reputation of the Seaford 'shags', the local coastguards and customs officers quickly arranged gangs of men to gather up the salvaged items and remove the remaining cargo from her hold. To necessitate this they built a wooden bridge with a double track laid along it for 'French Wagons' or trolleys to run on from the sea wall to the ship.

The cargo was then unloaded by means of block and tackle, and taken by farm carts to the railway station for transfer to London, or stored in the barn at Pigeon House Farm (near Sutton Road). Most of the cargo was out of the ship within three weeks, but en

The *Gannet* coming ashore at Seaford. The cargo was unloaded with the aid of block and tackle, and horses and carts stand by for loading. (By kind permission of Seaford Museum and Heritage Society)

The *Gannet* ashore and the sea breaking her up. (By kind permission of the Seaford Museum and Heritage Society)

route to the Pigeon Farm House some of the crates mysteriously disappeared thanks to the locals waiting at the roadside who used ropes to dislodge anything that had not been stacked securely. It is said that the local grocery shops had no call for tea or coffee for a while. Bad weather returned to Seaford on 1 March, with high seas breaking over the *Gannet* at a tremendous force and soon after 8a.m. she broke in two, spilling the contents of the cabins and saloon out. Sadly this was the beginning of the end for the *Gannet*: her funnel collapsed, the engines washed out onto the beach and slowly the sea reduced her to matchwood as many visitors from Lewes, Rottingdean and Eastbourne came to watch. Extended trains from Seaford were arranged in the evening to accommodate them all. For a number of years the *Gannet*'s keel was visible at low tide and in 1913 her propeller shaft was recovered by divers and displayed on the seafront.

A happy ending to the wreck of the *Gannet* that seems fitting as she came ashore on St Valentine's Day, was told to staff by descendents of a chambermaid from the Bay Hotel during a 'Ship Wreck' exhibition at Seaford Museum. It would appear that the captain rescued the ship's papers and brought them ashore soaking wet and one of the chambermaids helped him dry them. They fell in love, were married and went to India together on his next voyage.

Another victim of atrocious weather was the British sailing brig *Tally Ho* that left Sunderland at midday on Thursday 23 December 1886 with a cargo of 320 tons of coal, destined for Littlehampton. In command was master Joseph Gasston with a seven-man crew: James Scott (mate), Albert Greenyer (cook) and five seamen, Alfred Brown, William Young, Charles Leggett, David William Rumsey and James Mitchell. The *Tally Ho* was in safe hands as the experienced master had been on the vessel for sixteen years, and the *Tally Ho* had been overhauled at least twice, the last time only three weeks before this voyage.

Not long after leaving Sunderland she began to leak and throughout the voyage her pumps were used to keep the water level down. Weather conditions did not present problems for the crew, but as they came near to Hastings at around 2p.m. on Boxing Day she met a strong south-westerly wind with rain and mist. The *Tally Ho* tacked off to the south-east for two hours, then turned westwards but progress was difficult. The leak in the vessel became worse and despite the pumps being constantly manned, it was impossible to stem the flow of water. By 6p.m. the pumps became blocked with coal dust, and ceased to work efficiently, even though the crew worked them for a further two hours. By 7p.m. the *Tally Ho* was south-west of Royal Sovereign Light, about 18 miles from Newhaven, and as the conditions worsened Joseph Gasston decided to make for port, but soon realised it was impossible. Meanwhile William Young, who had been manning the pumps, informed the master that they were not working effectively, and asked what to do. Lost for an answer, the master suddenly caught sight of the lights of Eastbourne and took the decision to make for the town and beach the *Tally Ho*, so that he could at least save his crew. He scoured the area for the red light which stood on the Crumbles, a beach on the north-east side of Eastbourne town, knowing as he came close to the shoreline that the light marked the deepest water, which was used as a landing bay by fishermen. What Gasston didn't know was that the storm had blown out the light and what he could see were the gas lamps of the town. The waterlogged *Tally Ho* was making no headway in the gale – in fact she was being driven backwards – and by 10.15p.m. that evening, two hours from high tide, the tired, cold crew hauled a paraffin distress flare up onto the masthead as a night distress signal. This was seen by the coastguards at Eastbourne who in turn informed the officer in charge, Mr Angus Teeling, but, seeing an ordinary white light, he assumed that it was not a distress signal. The light suddenly went out and it was only then that the *Tally Ho* was seen broadside on about half a mile from the shore. Normally the coastguard would have sent a messenger to muster his men for the launch of the lifeboat, but realising the vessel was making for the shore, he ordered his men to go to the beach with lifelines.

The *Tally Ho* drifted through the waves and amazingly managed to clear the pier. With her sails still set and travelling at a great speed she eventually struck the beach with force at around 11p.m., 100 yards east of the Redoubt (a nineteenth-century fortification) with her bow pinned to a newly constructed groyne. As she beached the force of the sea turned the vessel broadside on, waves crashed over and rocked her from side to side, sending her mast, spars and rigging cascading onto the deck.

The crew were within metres of safety but at that point the beach steeped down to the water, preventing potential rescuers from reaching the vessel and the mariners from going ashore. Many spectators gathered on the shore in driving wind and rain and began calling for rocket lines to be used, echoed by the mariners calling for the rocket apparatus, but the nearest equipment was miles away at Belle Newhaven and Pevensey. With no rocket apparatus, and only the outline of the *Tally Ho* visible, the coastguards and lifeboat crew took on the extremely difficult task of throwing lifelines in the dark and windy conditions. Eventually after several attempts they were successful in getting one line on board. The first to use the lifeline was James Scott, who tied the line around himself, jumped into the water, and by using the rigging lying over the side of the vessel, made his way to the beach assisted by those ashore. William Young made an attempt to come ashore, but this time a heavier rope had been thrown on board with the intension of rescuing all the crew. However, when the rope landed on the vessel William hurriedly tied it around his body and jumped into the sea, shouting, 'I'm off,' against the advice of Master Gasston. In the darkness, those on the shore did not anticipate the line being used by one, so when it went taut, they assumed that it was being hauled onto the vessel, and by the time they realised what was happening it was too late. Young, who had injured himself, was dragged ashore, and carried up the beach. Despite the efforts of Dr J. Pitcairn-Brookless, a visitor to the town, and Dr Reid, who attempted to revive him with spirits and artificial respiration, they were unsuccessful and William Young was taken to the coastguard station where he died fifteen minutes later.

During the next half an hour three members of the crew, Alfred Thomas, Alfred Greenyer and Master Gasston, were safely brought ashore, but during the rescue, the

The *Tally Ho* aground at Eastbourne. (By kind permission of Eastbourne Library and David Renno)

master sustained a serious leg injury as he dropped from the deck. Two of the remaining crew, James Mitchell and Ordinary Seaman Charles Leggett, were washed overboard, one being seen clinging onto the rudder for a while before finally disappearing beneath the waves. The last member of the crew on the vessel, David William Rumney, clung to the bulwarks of the vessel and could be heard crying out, 'Save me, save me.' Lines were thrown within his reach, and one even fell over his shoulder, but he was too exhausted or numb to make that last physical effort to grasp the line. Finally, after hanging on for an hour, a succession of waves swept over him and he was drowned. The rescued were taken to the coastguard station where they were attended by the two doctors before the coastguards gave up their beds for the night.

The next day, Monday 17 December, brought a constant stream of people to the shore to view the *Tally Ho*. A collection was made at the wreck site and a small charge of 6d (2½p) was collected from anyone who wished to board the vessel, now high and dry at low water. A total of £18 11s ½d (£18.55) was collected for the families of the four men who died, a good sum in those days.

The following day the inquests into the deaths of the four crew members were held at the Hartington Hotel before the Coroner, Mr Hillam, with a jury consisting of mainly fishermen and boatmen, of whom the foreman was John Henry Wright. James Scott and Joseph Gasston were called as witnesses and outlined the tragic events. The next witness, Angus Teeling, the officer in charge of the local coastguard station, explained that the first light he saw on the *Tally Ho* was white and not blue. A verdict of accidental drowning was returned on each man, however the jury added a clause that the Board of Trade should be informed that, had a rocket apparatus been available at Eastbourne, the deceased would have been saved. The Board also stipulated that such apparatus should be installed at Eastbourne and the Council should be asked to provide red lights above the high water mark at the fishermen's cottages, as had such a light been installed it could have guided the master of the *Tally Ho*. On Monday 3 January 1887 a public auction was held for the sale of the hull, which was purchased by a Brighton man for £22, and 200 tons of coal, purchased for £125 by the Eastbourne Steam Laundry Company. At the Board of Trade enquiry held at the Shipwreck's Commissioner's Court in London on Tuesday 25 January 1887, it was revealed that the master, Joseph Gasston, did not have a master's certificate, but after hearing evidence from Mr Gates, the owner of the vessel, the court attached no blame to either the owners or the master. They found that the vessel was seaworthy, and that it was the severity of the gale on the night that caused the loss of both vessel and crew. The court also confirmed that had the vessel not been run ashore by the master then loss of life would have been even greater.

Some three years later, in the early hours of Thursday 24 April 1890, a thick fog blanketed the East Sussex coast waiting to claim another Sussex shipwreck. Making its way up the Channel was the *Polynesia*, a steamer travelling from Iquique in Chile to Hamburg in Germany with a cargo of nitrate of soda, worth £30,000. Master Reitman did not realise that the ship was so close to the shore and at 6.15a.m. it ran aground just to the west of Beachy Head, causing considerable damage to the hull. She began to fill

The *Tally Ho* was built at Shoreham in 1854 and beached at Eastbourne in 1886. (By kind permission of Marlipins Museum, Shoreham-by-Sea)

with water, and the pumps were manned to try to keep the water level down. News of her predicament did not reach Newhaven until about 10.40a.m. that morning and the Newhaven lifeboat *Michael Henry* was launched. The local Lloyd's agent Mr J. Bull also made his way to the scene on the steam tug *Tipper*, and found the *Polynesia* broadside on being driven further onto the rocks by a strong south-westerly wind and heavy seas. The lifeboat stood by until 4.30p.m. when the master decided the crew could do no more, and were transferred to the lifeboat and taken to Newhaven. However, the rescue boats were not the only crafts to visit the stricken *Polynesia*. The pleasure steamer *Nelson* came to view the scene from nearby Eastbourne with around 100 spectators on board. By 4.55p.m. the following day, the weather had abated sufficiently for the *Tipper* and the *Nelson* to return to the scene with a number of lighters, in the hope of salvaging the cargo, and pulling the vessel off the rocks. A number of the crew were brought back to the vessel to man the pumps as now there was about 8m of water inside her, and over the next few days the pumps were constantly manned whilst the nitrate of soda was removed and taken to Newhaven. The tugs were paid a sum of 15s (75p) a day to tow the lighters to Newhaven where the cargo was stored by the local railway company. By Sunday enough cargo had been removed for the Dover tug *Lady Vita* to attempt to pull the *Polynesia* off the rocks. This was partly successful in that the vessel was pulled clear of the rocks and towed towards Newhaven but, because she was taking in water so fast, she was beached at Cuckmere for more of her cargo to be offloaded.

On Tuesday 6 May the *Commerce* left Newhaven bound for Hamburg with 434 tons of the salvaged cargo, the remainder having been dissolved in the sea, so the local Lloyd's agent, having no further interest in the *Polynesia*, left her to the mercy of the sea and on 20 May a strong gale finally destroyed her. The stores and other equipment that were salvaged from the vessel and not returned to Hamburg on the *Commerce* were sold at auction on 24 May and realised a sum of £2,671 17s (£2,671.85).

One of the most noted shipwrecks of her time is the Danish iron barque *Peruvian* under the command of Master Norholm. She was 145 days into her voyage from Esmaralda in Ecuador to Hamburg with a cargo of logwood and palm seeds (ivory nuts which come from the South American palm and were used in the manufacture of buttons) when she foundered off Seaford on Wednesday 8 February 1899.

At around 3.10a.m. residents of Seaford were suddenly awoken by the sounds of rocket firing, a sound that only meant one thing, and they hurried to the shore where they found a three-masted sailing vessel stuck almost alongside the Esplanade Hotel. Shortly before 3a.m. a coastguard patrol reported to Chief Boatman Farrell at the Blatchington Coastguard Station that a vessel was firing distress signals. He answered the distress signal and contacted the Newhaven lifeboat *Michael Henry*, which was launched under the command of George Winter. Farrell gathered his men together and made for the vessel with the rocket apparatus. Eventually at the fourth attempt they secured a line to the vessel, and the lifeboat, powered only by oars, positioned itself between the ship and the beach and took on board the master, nine of the crew and the captain's dog. At the time the master assumed that all the ship's crew were aboard, and the lifeboat sent a signal to the coastguards that all the crew had been safely taken off the *Peruvian*. They were about to return to Newhaven when the master realised that his first and second mate were missing and called out several times to the missing crew, requesting they leave the vessel and board the lifeboat immediately. The lifeboat waited a further fifteen minutes before Coxswain Winter decided to make for the safety of Newhaven. Having received the signal that all was well, Chief Boatman Farrell and his men started to haul in their hawser, but realised that the line (known as the whip) was still on the *Peruvian*, which was now less than 100 yards from the shore. Suddenly they heard cries for help coming from the ship and realised that not all the crew were aboard the lifeboat. They could see no one, but out of the darkness came a faint voice, 'Pull away', and, as Farrell and his men began to pull on the line, they could see a man with a lifebelt around his waist coming through the sea to safety. He came ashore and explained that he was the second mate and had been below deck packing possessions. A further cry for help was heard, so again Farrell and his men tugged on the line and saw Neilson, the first mate, struggling through the surf without a lifebuoy. Unfortunately when he let go of the line to wade ashore he was hit by a huge wave that dragged him under the water and, although the coastguards rushed into the sea and grabbed him, he had already drowned.

An old postcard showing the Esplanade Hotel at Seaford.

The following morning, conditions were much calmer, so a salvage operation began to first remove the sails and spars, and then by midday it was intended to unload the cargo, prior to pulling the *Peruvian* into deeper waters to refloat her, but she was full of water. No doubt many residents were only too willing to help salvage the cargo and 'spirit' it away. Soon the palm seeds were washed ashore and the local residents were offered 2s (10p) for every hundredweight (51kg) they recovered from the beach. On the third day, Saturday, a gale came up from the south-west, and efforts to unload the cargo had to be abandoned. Large crowds gathered on the beach and along the Esplanade, but by 10p.m. the high tide smashed the vessel against the sea wall, with sparks flying against the dark sky, rather like fireworks, as the steel plates of the hull clashed. By midnight it was all over and the spectators watched as the *Peruvian* broke up. The same storm also took part of the sea wall opposite the Esplanade Hotel as it took the full force when the water rushed around the wreck.

By dawn on Sunday there was little left of the ship, although for many years the 'ivory nuts' could be found buried amongst the shingle. Local craftsmen created keepsakes of the shipwreck and these found their way into many of the Seaford homes, as the ivory nuts were turned into bottle pourers, and thimble cases. Others were polished smooth and an etching of the ship or the Seven Sisters worked onto the white surface of the shell and sold as souvenirs. Some of these can be seen in Seaford Museum, and Marlipins Museum, Shoreham-by-Sea, today.

The *Peruvian* coming ashore at Seaford watched by spectators. (By kind permission of Seaford Museum and Heritage Society)

The *Peruvian* ashore at Seaford in front of the Esplanade Hotel. (By kind permission of Newhaven Maritime Museum)

The *Peruvian* showing the remains of her bow at Seaford. (By kind permission of the Newhaven Maritime Museum)

Ivory nutshells from the *Peruvian*, which were decorated and sold as souvenirs. (By kind permission of Seaford Museum and Heritage Society)

More ivory nuts on display at Shoreham Museum. (Conrad Hughes, by kind permission of the Marlipins Museum, Shoreham-by-Sea)

Carved ivory nuts from the barque "Peruvian" which was wrecked off Seaford in 1899.

In 1984 one of the *Peruvian*'s iron catheads, the antenna-angled timbers for winding up the anchor cable and decorated with a lion's face, was raised and presented to Seaford Museum. A figurehead, thought to have been from the *Peruvian*, was recovered, and thought to represent Queen Anne, stood on the seafront at Seaford for many years and became very dilapidated. It was eventually given to Seaford Museum in 1984 and restored by David Taylor during 1986–87, who has made an excellent job of the restoration. The figurehead is interesting because originally it was crafted without a bolt or nail, and connects together purely by wooden pegs. A model of the figurehead can be seen in Seaford Museum today wearing two large gold necklaces, gold bracelets, and a gold tiara. Her long, flowing orange dress is trimmed with ostrich feathers held in place by a leather belt. She is also wearing what looks like a fur shawl, but on closer examination it is actually a lion's skin; the nose and paws of the animal are clearly seen. This could by a symbol of strength as the ship would have needed to be sturdy for her transatlantic voyages. She is also holding a piece of fruit to her breast, and the jewellery and ostrich feathers could be evidence of her trade along her South American routes.

On Wednesday 26 September 1900 the Norwegian barque *Sagatun*, under the command of Captain Simensen, had almost completed her voyage from Pited in Sweden to Newhaven with a cargo of timber, when a gale blew up in Seaford Bay. She anchored and rode out the storm for two days before breaking from her moorings and drifting ashore where she struck one of the groynes near the Esplanade Hotel. The captain, his fifteen-year-old daughter and a crew of nine were saved by rocket apparatus and the vessel was eventually sold and broken up. Local legend states that the capped gatepost at Sutton Mill was thought to have been the *Sagatun's* bowsprit.

The *Carnot*, a square-rigged schooner, left Boulogne on 25 November 1912, but almost immediately sailed into a storm, and had to put into Calais for a refit as her sails blew out. Almost four weeks later she set out again for St Malo carrying a crew of six consisting of Captain Bailbed, his mate named Arhan, two seamen, an apprentice and a cabin boy, together with the ship's pet dog, and a cargo of cement and herrings. Once again she was beaten back by several south-westerly gales which pushed her off course, until on 25 December a member of the crew spotted the St Catherine lighthouse on the tip of the Isle of Wight. On Boxing Day the mizzen mast broke and there was little chance of making any headway in the wind. Two days later her steering failed and the crew lost control of the *Carnot*, which sprang a leak and for the next hour all hands worked on the pumps to keep her afloat. That evening they finally saw the lights of a town on their right, and the captain ordered Arhan to check below where he found

Figurehead from the *Peruvian* before and after restoration. (By kind permission of Seaford Museum and Heritage Society)

The *Sagatun* ashore at Seaford. (By kind permission of Seaford Museum and Heritage Society)

the decks awash, the pumps chocked and the crew absolutely exhausted. The storm had actually pushed them north-east, in the opposite direction, and the town they saw was actually Bognor Regis. Around 10p.m. that night the ship went aground a mile from the shore at Aldwick and the crew immediately launched their small boat and eventually reached the shore, hauled their boat clear of the tide, and set out on foot in the direction of the lights of Bognor Regis.

A young woman answered a knock at the door at Goodman House, home of Mr New, and was surprised to find a man soaking wet and speaking in a foreign language with agitated gestures. Mr New telephoned the police station and Inspector Thomas and a constable set out for Goodman House. Walking in Steyne Street they came across three men, the captain and two of his crew, bare-footed, very wet and covered in sand. Despite the language problems the inspector gathered that they had been shipwrecked, and they all set off in the direction of the boat that brought them ashore. Meanwhile, down on the promenade, the local postman, Mr West, was taking advantage of the night air and saw three other sailors. When the inspector returned they were soon reunited with their fellow crew members and, on seeing the boat, was satisfied with their story. He then led them all back to Bognor Regis and took them to Louis Peacock in West Street, who could speak to them in French. Mr Peacock was able to piece their story together, and although it was now 11.30p.m., the policeman called on George Walters, the local secretary of the Shipwrecked Mariners' Society, who took the crew to the Pier Restaurant in Waterloo Square, where the owners, Mrs and Mrs Wall, made them some hot food and coffee before settling them down for the night. They also arranged

Wreck of the *Carnot* ashore at Aldwick, Bognor Regis. Men, women and children gather on shore to look at the French ship. (By kind permission of West Sussex County Council Library Service)

The French crew from the *Carnot*; three are enjoying a cigarette and one his pipe. (By kind permission of West Sussex County Council Library Service)

The SS *Brussels* wrecked near Southwick. (By kind permission of West Sussex County Council Library Service)

for a telegram to be sent to Captain Bailbed's home in St Malo confirming that he and his crew were safe. The ship's dog, a large black retriever, was put into the stables at Mr Peacock's home but it was so frightened it kept howling, so Mr Peacock brought it into the house where it went to sleep with its head on Mr Peacock's chest.

By now the *Carnot*, with some of its sail still raised, came ashore on the tide, and at around 2a.m. became stuck at the top of the beach on the very spot that the crew had landed. At 4a.m. the coastguard was informed that a vessel had run aground at Aldwick, and he was unsure whether the crew were safe or not. They passed the message to the coxswain and the secretary of the lifeboat who were unable to contact the windward lifeboat at Selsey, so called Littlehampton. Meanwhile the coastguard went to the beach where he found Mrs Croxton-Johnson, whose home was nearby, looking at the ship and he realised that because of its position the lifeboat was not needed, so the volunteer crew were informed that the vessel was well up the beach and the Felpham coastguard would board it. The next morning the Receiver of Wrecks arrived from Littlehampton and authorised the coastguard to take procession of the *Carnot* and her cargo. Spectators from Bognor Regis came to visit the wreck and take photographs, and on Monday morning when the *Carnot*'s hatches were opened, they were greeted with the delicious smell of cooked fish! The seawater had mixed with the cement and the heat generated had baked the salted herrings! Meanwhile the crew were enjoying the hospitality of the town, with Mr Peacock acting their interpreter. After finding them a set of clothing they were invited to tea with Mrs Croxton-Johnson and in the evening taken to a picture show at the Pier Theatre, where a collection took place which raised £2. Other donations amounted to another £2 4s (£2.40p). The following evening they were invited to a Christmas pantomime, 'Babes in the Wood', at the local Kursaal Theatre. When the French Consul arrived from Newhaven they took charge and arranged new clothes to be bought for each man from a shop in West Street, and returned them to St Malo on New Year's Day without Captain Bailbed, who owned the ship and remained behind. Attempts were made to refloat the *Carnot* on the spring tide, and to make this possible 160 tons of watered cement was removed, together with the 110 barrels of 'cooked' fish. Crowds of spectators gathered to watch the tug *Jumna* perform the operation. A cable was attached to the *Carnot* and, because of the rough seas, the *Jumna* hoisted a foresail to steady her, and while she got up to full power a gang of men were busy in the *Carnot* pumping water from her hull. Each wave lifted her stern a little, but after moving only a yard or so, she became lodged amidships against one of the wooden piles on the beach. Eventually the pile broke but the remaining stump still prevented further movement, despite all the tug's efforts. Further attempts to refloat her ended in failure and eventually the badly damaged hull

A stained-glass window by Chris Brown on Worthing Pier depicting wood that came ashore in 2008 from the *Ice Prince*. The window was commissioned by the Arts Council. (Conrad Hughes)

was auctioned on 27 January 1913. The remains of some solidified clumps of cement and the keel of the *Carnot* are still visible on the beach.

The SS *Brussels*, a single-funnel steamer owned by Messrs Rossiter and Holman of Devon, was pounded by heavy seas off Southwick on 5 July 1922 and ran aground on the shingle bar just inside Shoreham harbour with nine men aboard. It was en route from Caen, France to Shoreham with a cargo of artificial manure for Messrs John Brown & Sons of Shoreham when, on Tuesday 4 July, it ran into bad weather and decided to put into Littlehampton for the night. The following morning she continued her journey eastward and reached her destination a little later than planned. As she was making for the port a strong ebbing tide set in and she was driven off course, a little west of the harbour entrance. Eventually she headed for the haven but unfortunately her stern was caught by the tide and the steamer swung around and became broadside on to the shingle bar, where she lay for the rest of the day, blocking up the entrance. One of the crew had a lucky escape when a falling stanchion missed him, but all nine hands, including a sick man, were safely brought ashore and taken to the Seaman's Institute at Southwick where they were looked after by W.H. Preece, the Southwick missionary. The SS *Brussels* was reported to be in a serious condition with her back broken, but arrangements were made for an attempt to refloat her and bring her into port on the next high tide. Despite assistance from a tug it was realised that it would be impossible to move her from the entrance, and by high tide on the evening of Wednesday 5 July only her masts remained visible and she became a total wreck, with only one or two items being washed ashore.

In 2008 the *Ice Prince*, a Greek-registered cargo ship heading for Egypt, sank 26 miles off Portland Bill in Dorset. Although not a Sussex wreck, she shed 2,000 tonnes of timber, much of which was washed on to the beaches along the South Coast, from Ferring and Worthing to Newhaven and Seaford. One of the worst hit areas was Worthing, where a large quantity of timber was deposited on Worthing beach, which had to be closed to sightseers, to allow heavy machinery to remove the washed-up cargo, after they were warned that removing wood from the beach is against maritime law. At Newhaven the lifeboat was called out by a coastguard after a member of the public spotted what they thought was a body among the wood. It transpired that it was actually a survival suit believed to have come from the wrecked ship.

On 19 January 2009 a stained-glass window, in its glass partition, was unveiled on Worthing Pier. The specially commissioned window was created by local artist Chris Brown, and Worthing Arts Council also managed the 'Ice Prince Festival', marking the first anniversary of the shipwreck. Funding was granted through a well-publicised public competition, with a selection group including Arts Council representatives and members of Worthing Borough Council, who chose a variety of proposals covering as many art forms as possible, focusing on bringing new art in many forms to the town.

Five

EQUIPMENT, LIFEBOATS AND COASTGUARDS TO THE RESCUE

THE COASTGUARD service was not formed until 1822, but there were those who were saddened by the loss of life, and set about helping those in danger, the first being Captain George Manby, who invented the Manby rocket apparatus in 1807. He was born in 1765 at Downham Market in Norfolk and was a boyhood friend of Lord Nelson. He found that by using a brass mortar it was possible to fire a weight attached to a line a distance of up to 275 yards onto a floundering ship. A piece of plaited hide was placed between the shot and the line to prevent it from being burnt when the shot was fired, and in 1821 the idea was modified to enable the line to travel further and was extensively used by those rescuing the shipwrecked around our coasts. Captain Manby was well respected for his work, and on 12 May 1831 was elected a Fellow of The Royal Society in London.

The breeches buoy was another piece of equipment that was used to good effect, and was invented by Admiral Kisbee and first exhibited at the Paris Exhibition in 1854. It operates by fixing a line from the rescue rocket to the wreck's mast, and the breeches buoy, like a canvas bucket hanging from a cork float, was sent across. There were two holes in the bottom of the bucket and the seaman sat inside with his feet dangling through the holes. He was lowered over the side of the wreck and hauled to safety by the shore crew. In rough seas he would often be down in the waves, where the cork float helped keep his head clear of the water and stopped him from drowning.

Another piece of equipment that was used along our shores, especially between Newhaven and Beachy Head, was the cliff-top rescue crane. Made of wood, the crane included a ballast counterweight at the rear, which enabled the jib to reach 12ft out into the sea from the cliff face. A wicker basket, used for rescuing shipwrecked sailors, was fitted with a wire floor to reduce the wind difference. A model of the rescue crane based on plans and photographs dating from 1842 can be seen at Newhaven Museum.

Coastguard firing a rocket, as used in various rescues in this book. (By kind permission of Tony Daly)

Cliff top Rescue Crane

The model is based on plans from 1842 and photographs from the 1880's. Ballast counterweight at the rear enabled the jib to reach 12 ft out from the cliff face. The wicker basket had a wire floor to reduce wind [resista]nce. Scale 1:25

Model of a cliff-top rescue crane on display at Newhaven Museum. (Conrad Hughes, by kind permission of the Newhaven Maritime Museum)

Thursday 16 December 1869 started out pleasant as far as December days go with a calm sea, and no doubt the people of Seaford went about their daily business without a care in the world, but by noon, the chilly wind had freshened increasing through the day until, by 7.30p.m., it reached gale force with high seas and driving rain.

Off the coast of Seaford, on the horizon appeared the *Seraphina*, or as some newspapers reported her, the *Seraphine*, or *Sepaphim*. She left Caen for Swansea with a cargo of stone and it was not known whether it was ballast or for building. The master, Mr Langris, and his eight-man crew were French, consisting of ship's mate Runguard, Octamori, Silvade, Forriere, Romani, Locture, Maran and an unknown boy. In these appalling conditions, the *Seraphina* tried to make for the safety of Newhaven harbour, but as she approached the crew found her difficult to manage and she was driven past the mouth of the harbour, coming ashore to the east with the vessel being pushed halfway up the beach.

A local fisherman, George Green, saw *Seraphina* was in trouble and, fearing she would be driven ashore, immediately raised the alarm. Many residents soon came down to the shore and, as it was a bright moon, they could see the full scenario, but no one could get close enough to help.

Richard Mallett, chief boatman with the coastguard station at Blatchington, arrived on the scene, and luckily for the crew of the *Seraphina* had a small boathouse close by where he stored his fishing gear. He grabbed a rope, tied it around his waist and handed the other end to those on the shore. Without a thought for his own safely he rushed into the raging sea taking a line with him and managed to attach it to the vessel, remaining in the sea close to the hull to help the crew go ashore one by one, so saving their lives. Unfortunately the young lad, who had only been at sea a few days, did the same as the others, making his way hand over hand along the line, but suddenly lost his grip and a huge wave carried him into the sea. He threw his arms in the air several times but then disappeared and was lost.

The rescued crew were taken to the New Inn where the owner, Mrs Simpson, gave them dry clothing before they were looked after by Mr Walter Towner, the secretary of the local Shipwrecked Mariners' Society. Unfortunately the crew lost everything, including a box containing 3,000 francs in banknotes belonging to the master.

Arrangements were made by Mr Black, vice consul at Brighton, and Mr Dolan, Receiver of Wrecks at Newhaven, for the crew to board a vessel at Newhaven on Saturday 18 December bound for France, no doubt relieved, after their ordeal, to be spending Christmas with their families.

Richard Mallett already had a distinguished career in the navy where he gained a reputation for lifesaving, but he was no stranger to local rescues. One crew member was rescued from the wreck of the brig *Woodside* in the bay in 1860, and two years later he ran into the sea, risking his own life, to throw a line on board the French schooner *Jean Albert* and saved all the crew after the ship beached in a gale at Seaford. For this act of gallantry he was promoted to chief boatman, but his greatest achievement was for his help to the *Seraphina*. He was awarded the Royal Humane Society's bronze medal and a gold medal (first class) from the French government for his efforts in saving the crew. He was also presented with a watch and chain paid for by a local collection that had been organised by Mr Henry Blyth. The remainder of the collection, £8 7s 11½d (£8.38p), was shared among those who helped with the rescue. Richard Mallett is remembered today in Mallett Close, just behind the Esplanade in Seaford, within sight of his gallant deeds of courage.

On 3 October 1883 the *New Brunswick*, a Norwegian three-masted sailing barque, left Quebec for West Hartlepool, carrying a cargo of timber. All was well until she reached the English Channel and ran into a south-westerly gale. The vessel was driven before the storm over the next few days, during which time her sails were ripped to pieces and her topmasts carried away. She continued to be battered by hurricane-force winds near to Beachy Head and at dawn on Sunday 25 November 1883 was driven helplessly closer to the cliffs.

The master, P. Tobisen, in an attempt to stop her from drifting even closer, dropped her two anchors but, in these dreadful conditions, it was not long before the anchors began to drag and the vessel drifted towards the rocks, eventually stopping 1km from the shore just east of Birling Gap. The crew on the *New Brunswick* quickly hoisted distress signals that were picked up by the local coastguards. To the relief of the crew a crowd gathered on the beach although there was no way to communicate with them. Meanwhile, large waves continued to wash over the vessel so, to prevent them from being washed overboard, the crew of ten lashed themselves to the remaining rigging.

By 10.45a.m. news of the *New Brunswick* had reached Eastbourne, just as the Mayor and the Corporation were leaving the Vestry Hall for the Mayor's Sunday parade. Alderman Rudd and Councillor Thomas Bennett, agent and sub-agent of Lloyd's, left the parade and sent a telegram to Newhaven as they thought the Newhaven lifeboat would get there quicker. However, after further discussions, the local honorary secretary of the RNLI and Charles Hide, coxswain of the lifeboat, decided that it was unsafe for the Newhaven lifeboat to leave harbour. The Eastbourne lifeboat crew mustered at their station, and *William and Mary*, a self-righting sailing boat with ten oars, prepared for the rescue. Unfortunately the winds and mounting seas made it impossible for the lifeboat to clear the harbour, and the steam tug *Tipper*, usually used to tow the lifeboat, was not prepared as it would have taken far too long to get sufficient steam up. The decision was taken then to haul the lifeboat overland to Birling Gap and launch from there. It was placed on its wheeled carriage, and the crew, together with around 200 willing volunteers, manually hauled the carriage up South Street where the first team of six horses were attached. In driving rain and wind another four horses were added for the steep climb up the newly constructed Duke's Drive, then across ploughed fields for 5 miles to the Gap. However, they found the cutting to the beach too narrow for the carriage wheels to pass through as the rough sea had washed away the lower 10ft of the path. They improvised by making a slipway from timber found nearby, and at 1.15p.m. the *William and Mary* was launched. In the violent storm, the lifeboat crew, in their cork jackets, rowed towards the *New Brunswick*, but it took nearly an hour to reach the vessel with water having to be constantly pumped from the lifeboat as each wave broke. Once they were close enough to the vessel the lifeboat crew threw a rope, and once attached, the crew dropped into the sea, one by one, to be hauled safely on to the lifeboat. By 4.30p.m. it was all over and everyone was back at Birling Gap. Only one crew member was injured, with two crushed ribs, and he was taken to a nearby cottage belonging to the coastguard, and attended to by a doctor. The lifeboat crew and the volunteers were left with the task of putting the lifeboat onto the carriage and hauling it back the way they came, but not before they were given bread, meat and ale from the Devonshire Hotel. They finally arrived back at 7.30p.m. that evening. The *New Brunswick*'s anchor held and so, the next day, the steam tug *Tipper* was able to refloat her and tow her safely into port. Charlie Hide was the local hero of the day, but he and other crew members of the lifeboat made a claim for the 'salvage' of the ship, in contravention of RNLI rules. The argument dragged on with much ill-feeling on both sides but the owners of the Norwegian barque paid up and sadly the Lifeboat Institution, with great reluctance, had to dismiss the entire Eastbourne lifeboat crew. A rather sad ending to a very brave rescue, I think.

According to the *Argus* newspaper, the morning of 14 November 1894 was a foul one, and hundreds of local people had gathered on East Worthing's seafront to watch as the gale brought waves crashing on to the shingle with an almighty roar. On the horizon the spectators spotted a ship's lifeboat, and made out the figure of one solitary man at the tiller. They later discovered he was the sole survivor from the *Zadne*, a 490-ton steamship carrying a cargo of coal from South Wales to London. Just metres from the shore spectators watched in horror as the lifeboat flipped over and the man was thrown into the sea and drowned. What happened on board the *Zadne* in those fateful last hours remains a mystery, and some even criticised the failure of the town's lifeboat to launch. The *Sussex Daily News* reported:

> The small knot of spectators at the pier head was, perhaps the first to catch sight of a small speck, through the surf, some quarter of a mile to the east. Residents of the Half Brick public house saw from their upper windows the man standing alone in the little craft, endeavouring to steer his boat to take the enormous seas which threatened each moment to overwhelm him.

Over the next few days eleven bodies from the *Zadne* were washed ashore and taken to the mortuary in the High Street, prior to the inquest at the Anchor Inn, now the Jack Horner. All the bodies came ashore within half a mile of each other, suggesting they had all died in shallow water, implying that they may have got into the vessel's lifeboats before *Zadne* sank, but the truth of what happened to the vessel and its crew will never be known.

The newspaper reports were graphic in detail:

Blood in many places has been drawn freely and, except in one case, no limbs appear to have been broken, although the force of the waters has torn the clothing of several into shreds, leaving the cut and horribly disfigured limbs exposed.

At the inquest the man in the lifeboat was described as around twenty-two years of age with light brown hair, a slight moustache, grey eyes, plus tattoos on the left forearm with the letters V U, and an anchor in blue and red and a ship in full sail. The other victims were: Master Thomas Farrel; First Mate George Tosh; Second Mate George Dunn; Steward C. Erickson; E.J. Sweeney, John Sullivan, Frank Kinsella and E. Frank (all able seamen); First Engineer D.S. Henderson; Second Engineer Frederick William Strange; Donkeyman T.J. Farrell; J. Gordon, T. Steer and J. Leisk (all firemen); and two others who could not be identified. All except one is buried at Broadwater cemetery, and the funeral was attended by several thousand people who lined the route of the procession, led by the Salvation Army Band. It was described as 'an impressive and pathetic sight'. The other body was taken back to South Wales for interment.

The Royal National Lifeboat Institute held an inquiry into the loss of the *Zadne* in which Charles Lee, the coxswain, informed them that the crew had been ready to go out but visibility was no more than 300 yards. The RNLI agreed the tragedy had unfolded out of sight and by the time the crew became aware of the situation it was too late. They concluded that there was no failure of duty by the Worthing lifeboat crew.

Two years later, on Sunday 6 December 1896, the Norwegian three-masted barque *Ophir* was in distress in the same area and ran aground in heavy seas off Lancing. As day broke, her distress signals were picked up by the coastguards at Worthing, Lancing and Shoreham, and she was seen struggling in heavy seas. The ten-man crew had cut down the main and mizzen masts to prevent her from keeling over, but were unable to get them clear of the rigging, and they lay tangled in a heap near the stern. The chief officer of Lancing coastguard informed the coastguard station at Worthing and the lifeboat station at Shoreham. Just after 8a.m. Chief Officer Lang of the Worthing coastguard ordered the Worthing lifeboat to go out, and the maroon was fired to summon the crew, but it also woke residents who hurried down to the shore to watch the rescue. The *Ophir* was near to the shore at Lancing, but Lancing Road was impassable as the sea had washed over it, so the Worthing lifeboat *Henry Harris* was launched from Worthing. It took two attempts to launch her as the breakers were strong, but Coxswain Lee and the crew pulled hard on the oars and, once beyond the breakers, were able to hoist the sails. The Shoreham crew were not so lucky; their oars snapped and they were beaten back by the strong waves. The Worthing crew battled on, and an hour and half later dropped anchor alongside the *Ophir*. It would have been easier to rescue the crew from the stern end, but as there was so much debris from the masts Coxswain Lee was forced to steer the *Henry Harris* around to the windward side. Communication was difficult

The *Ophir* in shallow waters after being driven aground on 6 December 1896. (Walter Gardiner Photography Collection, by kind permission of West Sussex County Council Library Service)

as the crew of the *Ophir* only spoke Norwegian, but eventually they understood and ropes were thrown and fastened to the ship. A breeches buoy was rigged up and the rescue began. The first to be rescued was the ship's steward who had apparently been ill for many weeks, and then the ship's mate before the *Ophir* was driven away from the lifeboat ending up just 100 yards from the beach. The *Henry Harris* attempted to approach from the windward side three more times, but was forced to pull away for fear of being smashed against the *Ophir*. By now Shoreham coastguards had arrived and quickly prepared their rocket apparatus and at the third attempt it reached its target, much to the delight of the gathering spectators. However, it was soon realised that the line was either broken or too short, so a fourth was fired, and successfully secured to the ship. One by one the eight remaining men were pulled along the line until all reached safety, although one almost didn't make it because he was numb with cold and found it difficult to hold on. Hanging face downwards, the cord caught around his neck, and his hands prevented the pulley block from moving. When the rescuers realised what was happening Mr Davey, boatman at Worthing coastguard, and William Dart, boatman of Lancing coastguard, rushed into the sea to untangle him and prevent him from death by drowning or strangulation. The crew were taken to the Three Horseshoes

Ophir Road, in Worthing, named after the ship that ran aground in 1896. (Conrad Hughes)

Inn nearby where they were cared for by Mr F. Parish, a surgeon, whilst accommodation was arranged by Chief Officer Lang of Lancing coastguard, who also happened to be the local agent for the Shipwrecked Mariners' Society. The lifeboat crew rowed back to Worthing with the two seamen they had rescued, but the steward, who had been in the lifeboat for three hours, became delirious. Coxswain Lee tried to land him on the pier, but the high sea made it impossible, so they waited hoping the storm would calm down, but they were forced to bind the steward with rope as he was thrashing around like a madman. The *Henry Harris* neared the pier once more, and this time eager hands plucked him from the boat, placed him in a bath chair and wheeled him to the pier entrance where Mr Parish, who had travelled from Lancing, took him to the infirmary. The ship's mate finally came ashore at 2.30p.m., and was taken to the Three Horseshoes Inn where he joined his fellow crew members. The Worthing lifeboat crew of thirteen returned to the lifeboat house at 3p.m., and their efforts were not forgotten. Each received 15s from the Institution's funds and forty-six people who helped haul and launch the *Henry Harris* were awarded 4s 6d each.

The *Ophir* remained upright on the shore and many people came to look at her, picking their way through the mud and shingle that had washed ashore. However, no one was allowed on board, but to everyone's amazement they saw a dog running around the deck, then a goat, and finally a cat. On Monday morning, as soon as the sea subsided, Lancing coastguards took Captain Julius Olsen aboard to retrieve the animals, the sailors' belongings and the ship's papers. The captain, who spoke good English, explained that the *Ophir*, owned by a Mr Pettersen of Arendal in Norway, was returning home from Trapani in Sicily with a cargo of salt, but it had all washed out through a damaged hole in the ship. She had left the Sicilian port on 28 September, but the voyage, which normally took thirty days, had taken seventy-eight by the time she had come to grief. The sailors stayed at the inn until Friday, before being taken to London and shipped home to Norway. The captain remained at the inn, pending the sale of the vessel which was auctioned on Thursday 17 December, just ten days after being wrecked. It was sold to a Mr Read for only £34, the four small boats and five sails went for £2 each, whilst Captain Olsen successfully bid for the chronometer at £4 10s. As for the sick steward, he remained in the infirmary until Christmas and returned to Norway with Captain Olsen. In appreciation for his hospitality, the captain gave the goat to the landlord of the inn, and asked him to look after his cat and dog until a permanent home could be found for both. The name of the ship lives on today in Ophir Road on the seafront at East Worthing.

One of three capstans on Worthing beach surviving from the nineteenth century. (Conrad Hughes)

Worthing's Old Coastguard
House in Marine Parade,
overlooking the sea.
(Conrad Hughes)

Worthing's lifeboat station,
with its conical lookout
tower. (Conrad Hughes)

Sadly sometimes those who go to the aid of others end up losing their lives, which is what happened in the *Mary Stanford* lifeboat disaster when her entire crew of seventeen was lost. The tragedy began early on 15 November 1928, when a south-westerly gale with winds gusting over 80mph ravished the English Channel, finding many ships in difficulties, although most found their way to shelter. At 5a.m. the maroons were fired, informing the crew on the troubled *Alice of Riga* that help was on its way. The Latvian vessel had been in collision with a large German cargo ship, *Smyrna*, a little out of the area of this book at Dungeness. The *Alice of Riga* had lost her rudder in the collision, was holed taking in water, and drifting helplessly. Those helping the crew to launch the lifeboat struggled in the wind to get to the lifeboat house, situated 1¼ miles from Rye harbour. After three attempts the *Mary Stanford*, a non-self-righting fourteen-oar boat was launched around 6.45a.m. Five minutes later Rye coastguards received a message that the crew on the *Alice of Riga* were safe and had been rescued by the *Smyrna* and the lifeboat was no longer needed. Despite efforts to inform the lifeboat by flare that they were not needed, the crew were too busy coping with the spray and rain that they did not see the recall signal. The mate on the SS *Halton* reported that he saw the lifeboat 3 miles west-south-west from Dungeness and everything appeared to be fine; a little later on a young sailor on the *Smyrna* saw the lifeboat. Cecil Marchant, who was collecting driftwood at Camber saw the vessel capsize, ran home to tell his parents, and felt a clout for making up stories, but his father thought that perhaps he should report it to the coastguards at Camber. Soon rumours spread around the seafaring community that the lifeboat had gone under, and official confirmation came at midday as the *Mary Stanford* was seen bottom up, drifting towards the shore. It is said that over 100 men rushed to the shore where the lifeboat finally come to rest, and every effort possible was used to try and revive fifteen of the crew that were washed ashore, but none could be saved and after two hours the bodies were taken to Lydd for identification. Over the days that followed the disaster the newspapers, national and local, carried the story, and rumours as to why it happened were rife, including one, wrongly assumed, that the lifejackets had become waterlogged and the weight had dragged the crew under. The community was devastated as most of the crew had grown up and worked together. Eighteen dependent wives and parents were left, and eleven children were left fatherless. They were also buried together following a mass funeral, held on 20 November, but two of the crew members' bodies had not been found in time for the funeral. Three months later the body of Henry Cutting was washed ashore at Eastbourne, but the body of the youngest member of the crew, seventeen-year-old John Head, the coxswain's son, was never found. Hundreds of people attended the funeral, including members of the Latvian government, because the men had lost their lives going to the assistance of the Latvian vessel. A Court of Enquiry sat for three days in December and on the first three days in January 1929 and came to the conclusion that as there were no survivors the cause of the capsizing was a matter of conjecture. From the evidence available they concluded that, whilst attempting to make the harbour on a strong tide, in dangerous

The *Mary Stanford* Memorial at Rye harbour. (Photograph by Conrad Hughes)

weather conditions, the *Mary Stanford* suddenly capsized and the crew were thrown into the water. Two of the crew were entangled under the boat. The empty *Alice of Riga* drifted towards the shore at Dungeness where she broke up and sank. Her crew were put ashore at Antwerp in Belgium when the storm subsided. The *Mary Stanford* was eventually taken to the RNLI depot in London where she was dismantled and broken up. The lifeboat house was closed as a mark of respect and was never used again. Today a fine memorial to the men can be seen at Rye harbour. It was presented by the people of the Isle of Man and is made of Manx stone. Above the statue of a lifeboatman are the words: 'We have done that which was our duty to do.' A very fitting memorial I feel. There is also a stained-glass window in Winchelsea Church depicting a lifeboat putting out to a ship in distress, while figures on the shore watch.

Just before midday on Sunday 29 July 1956, the Selsey lifeboat rescued eighteen people from three yachts, and their coxswain, Douglas Grant, was later awarded the silver medal. It all began when the local coastguard reported that a small yacht had been sighted flying a distress signal. The maroons were fired and the lifeboat crew hurried down to the boathouse in winds of 60mph sweeping along the gangway leading out to the boathouse. At 12.10p.m. the *Canadian Pacific* slid down the slipway into the raging sea. When the lifeboat reached the area to the east of Selsey Bill they met lobster pots drifting in their path, and soon both propellers were fouled up, reducing the revs on the engine. In such heavy seas it was impossible to stop the engines to clear the propellers, so the lifeboat battled on. Twenty minutes later the Dutch-built boeier *Maasult* was sighted. She had lost her sails and was yawing wildly, her engines still working. She was almost surrounded by rocks and, even though visibility was poor, Coxswain Grant slowly manoeuvred the lifeboat up to the *Maasult* but, just as the two boats came together, a huge wave swept the vessel away from the lifeboat. At that moment the lifeboat crew spotted another yacht, the *Bloodhound*, which appeared to be in much greater danger than the *Maasult*, so Coxswain Grant headed in her direction. Huge waves swept over her threatening to wash the crew overboard. Coxswain Grant skilfully moved the lifeboat up to the yacht and held her there bow on, by using the engine and the rudder. The sea continued to wash over both the boats as seven men and two women were rescued from the *Bloodhound*, and once everyone was aboard the lifeboat the coxswain reversed both engines to pull clear. The manoeuvre helped clear some of the rope tangled in her propellers, and as a result power increased. The nine survivors were placed in the lifeboat's cabin wrapped in blankets as Coxswain Grant headed back to the *Maasult*. Thankfully she had not drifted too far and the lifeboat was able to approach from the weather side, but the leeboards on the vessel made it difficult for the lifeboat to get alongside and so it had to be driven in over the low bulwarks of the vessel and held there by the engines. All six on board, three men, a woman, a twelve-year-old girl and a twenty-two-month-old baby were rescued thanks to the skill of Coxswain Grant, and soon after the *Maasult* disappeared. The owner later said that as the lifeboat approached his anemometer registered a wind speed of over 90mph, and estimated the breaking waves were 30ft high. During the rescues the lifeboat suffered some slight damage and the rudder jammed. As there was a possibility that the lifeboat would be driven ashore, the order was given to, 'Drop anchor'. Just as the coxswain was about to shout, 'Let go', the rudder freed itself from what may have been a fishing float or a lobster pot, and Coxswain Grant set the course for Portsmouth harbour. Soon the crew of the lifeboat spotted yet another yacht, the *Coima*, on its beam-end, having been driven by the storm from anchorage at St Helen's Roads and in danger of being swept ashore. Yet again the coxswain moved the lifeboat up to *Coima*'s starboard-quarter and the crew of three came aboard, just before the yacht sank. After landing all eighteen survivors safely at Portsmouth the lifeboatmen had a hot meal before returning to Selsey. The following morning, after a good night's sleep, they went out again and towed in the *Bloodhound* which had managed to survive the storm.

For their efforts Coxswain Grant was awarded a silver medal, and each of the other crew members, Second Coxswain Len Lawrence, Bowman H. Lawrence, Motor Mechanic John Haslett, Assistant Mechanic A. Fullick and Lifeboatmen J. Byron, J. Woodland and K. Laidment were awarded the RNLI thanks on vellum. In 1983 divers found a wreck and, by the bell, identified it as the *Maasult*.

Eendracht ashore at Seaford in 1998, after fifty youngsters were airlifted to safety. (By kind permission of Seaford Museum and Heritage Society)

Eendracht caught in the shingle at Seaford. (By kind permission of Seaford Museum and Heritage Society)

In more recent times Seaford woke to one of the biggest air/sea rescues of modern days. The three-masted Dutch training ship the *Eendracht*, bound for Ostend, had put into Newhaven harbour for the night, with a crew of fifty young sailors on board. The following morning she left the harbour at 8a.m., and for some reason became stuck on a sandbank and ran aground off the East Pier after being battered by 20ft waves and suffering engine failure. At 8.30a.m. the 35m vessel had made it as far as the lighthouse at the end of the breakwater before the wind turned her to port and she became beached lying on her side. The Newhaven lifeboat, and the tug *Meeching*, tried to attach a line to the vessel in an attempt to pull her upright, but it proved impossible with the heavy sea. Paramedics and police stood by, whilst overhead, the coastguard helicopters India Juliet and Hotel Lima hovered. On shore, hundreds of spectators waited with baited breath as the crew were winched to safety in a dramatic air and sea rescue, and taken to the P&O Stena ferry terminal at Newhaven to recover from their ordeal. Only one person sustained minor injuries and was taken to Brighton's County Hospital, but was later discharged and joined the rest of the crew, being cared for by the local authorities. According to an article in the *Seaford Gazette* dated 28 October 1998, the raging wind sent a torrent of salty water crashing down on the stranded crew, whilst on the beach rescuers shielded their faces from the biting spray. Dave Kyte, a licensed boatman running chartered vessels out of Newhaven, raced to the scene and later said, 'For people who go to sea it was quite an emotional experience to see a boat stricken like that. It's a mixture of sadness it's happened, relief that everyone got off safely and the fact that it could happen to anyone.'

The next day a mechanical digger was brought in to shift some of the shingle and many people were present to witness the *Eendracht* finally being refloated at 1.45p.m. on the Friday before being towed to Dover by the Newhaven tug *Lady Hamilton*.

Six

ON COURSE FOR COLLISION

WITHOUT THE help of today's navigational equipment, it was inevitable that ships would collide, especially in adverse conditions, and the first one in this chapter is the Spanish sailing barque *Vizcaya*, which collided with the Dutch ship *D'Elmira* off Beachy Head. The *Vizcaya* was returning to Bordeaux from London in ballast when the collision happened during the early hours of 1/2 February 1859, in a south-westerly gale and high seas. The crew on the *Vizcaya*, thinking that she was about to go down as her sides were stoved and her rigging and little boats were smashed, managed to get aboard the *D'Elmira*. She had been en route from Batavia to Rotterdam and was so badly damaged that she was forced to fire a distress signal that was picked up by the tug *Don*, which then towed the stricken *D'Elmira* to Portsmouth from where the crew of the *Vizcaya* later travelled to Newhaven by rail. The *Vizcaya* was left abandoned to the elements, her rigging in a tangle on deck, and later that morning she was spotted drifting down the Channel off the coast of Brighton by the Rottingdean coastguard. Lifeboats from both Brighton and Newhaven were launched together with a four-oared coastguard galley from Rottingdean. The first to arrive on the scene was the Rottingdean coastguard galley which, after a great deal of struggling, managed to anchor the totally deserted ship. Next to arrive was the Brighton lifeboat but the crew on the Rottingdean galley declined any help, no doubt hoping to claim the salvage money for themselves, but upon leaving they requested from Newhaven that an available steamer should to sent to help. Soon the Brighton & South Coast Railway steamer *Lyons* arrived and with some difficulty the *Vizcaya* was finally attached to a hawser, and brought safely into Newhaven harbour. Later, at a hearing, the Admiralty Court awarded £250 to the *Lyons*, £150 to the Rottingdean coastguard and £100 to Newhaven lifeboat. The wreck was later bought and re-rigged by a Littlehampton man, Mr J. Robinson, but

Vizcaya being towed back to Newhaven harbour after she was mysteriously found off Rottingdean.
(By kind permission of Newhaven Museum)

unfortunately she was wrecked off the Norfolk coast in 1893, in ballast, on a voyage
from Littlehampton to the Tyne.

The *Vandalia*, a wooden sailing ship, was on a voyage from New York to London
with a cargo of refined petroleum in barrels, when it appears she collided with the
Duke of Buccleugh after not observing the rule requiring the *Vandalia* to give way on
her starboard side, and sank on the night of 8 March 1889 with all hands. The *Vandalia*
continued to sail with massive damage to her bows and eventually beached in shallow
water off Brighton and broke up. The captain of the *Vandalia* lied about the collision
and told the court of enquiry that the steamer had rammed him head on and proceeded
on her way, and although some wreckage came ashore, nothing was heard of the *Duke
of Buccleugh* or its crew.

In 1990 the wreck of the *Duke of Buccleugh* was found by chance when a group of
expert divers from Littlehampton came across her whilst looking for another wreck.
She was found to be upright and almost intact with her masts lying across her. She had a
huge split in the starboard side close to the bridge and about 180ft back from the bow. A
china plate with the words 'Ducal Lines' printed around a crown motif was the first clue
of her identity and was from the goods destined for the hotel trade in India. Originally
she carried 600 tons of hand-painted Belgian porcelain, china and glassware, much of
which is now broken. Also on board were 2,533 tons of iron rails and machinery, also
destined for Madras.

An etching of the *Vandalia* wrecked at Brighton after being abandoned by her crew in 1889, after she was in collision with the *Duke of Buccleugh* off Selsey Bill. (By kind permission of Marlipins Museum, Shoreham-by-Sea)

The steamer SS *Seaford* was the pride and joy of the London, Brighton & South Coast Railway Company, and the first passenger ship in the fleet to be driven by twin screws instead of paddles. She cost £57,500 to build and was launched at the builder's shipyard on the Clyde on 19 April 1894. Thirty-six-year-old Richard Sharp, the company's most senior master, who had been with the company for fourteen years, was appointed her master, and the ship served regularly between Newhaven and Dieppe with an average journey time of three hours and twenty-one minutes. She was licensed to carry 775 passengers. The Chinese government were so impressed with her speed that upon the outbreak of war with Japan, they offered a large sum of money for her, far more than she was worth, but the offer was refused.

Almost a year after her launch, on Wednesday 21 August 1895 at 1.25p.m., the SS *Seaford* left Dieppe on her regular passenger service crossing to Newhaven with 255 passengers and a crew of forty-one under the command of Richard Sharp. Off Beachy Head she hit dense fog and the master took charge of the vessel and reduced speed. As the fog worsened he reduced the speed further, but Richard Sharp could not help feeling a little apprehensive as he stood on the bridge. The ship's fog siren constantly sounded but no one responded. Then, after about thirty minutes, in the distance a feeble response was heard and suddenly the steamship *Lyons* emerged on the port side from the fog, less than a ship's length away. The *Lyons*, under the command of Captain Gauvin, was a cargo steamer, owned by the same company and had left Newhaven for Dieppe that afternoon and would have been aware that the SS *Seaford* should be on her return voyage. Sharp immediately gave the order to put the engines in reverse, and helm to starboard. Captain Gauvin did likewise but it was too late, the two ships collided. The *Lyons* struck the SS *Seaford* amidships, and the crew on the bridge were thrown to the ground. Captain Sharp got up and ordered that a survey of the ship be carried out. Although both ships had been travelling at a very slow speed, both were damaged, but it was the SS *Seaford* that took the brunt of the impact. The decking had been ripped up and timber and glass littered the deck, with the dining area faring the worst where many passengers were eating lunch. Below the waterline the SS *Seaford* suffered a large gash, and it was obvious the vessel was sinking. Richard Sharp's thoughts were for his passengers and he ordered the issue of SS *Seaford*'s lifebelts and lowered the lifeboats. Meanwhile the *Lyons* limped around with her pumps working at full power to remove the water entering the damaged bow and to keep her afloat. Sharp gave the order for the passengers on the SS *Seaford* to be transferred to the *Lyons*, and most of the passengers managed to climb aboard the *Lyons* without incident. However, one, a Mrs Pearslow, lost her grip and fell between the two ships and, although in danger of being crushed, was kept afloat by her lifebelt until she was quickly rescued, by the SS *Seaford*'s second officer, and only sustained a broken ankle. Another passenger, Charles Pickard from Versailles, broke his leg on impact, and two other ladies also broke limbs. Once on board the *Lyons* the passengers were kept at the stern of the ship to keep as much weight as possible from her damaged bow and made as comfortable as possible. When Captain Sharp was certain all 255 passengers were safe, he and several members of the SS *Seaford*'s crew boarded the two lifeboats and, in keeping with tradition, was the last to leave his ship. With all passengers safely on board, the *Lyons* towed the boats containing the SS *Seaford*'s crew back to Newhaven. Just twenty-five minutes after the rescue of the passengers and crew the SS *Seaford* disappeared from sight, stern first, and was never seen again. There was no time to save any of the passengers' belongings and it was reported that it was thanks to the prompt action by the chief engineer, Mr Moneypenny, who closed all the watertight doors on the SS *Seaford*, that so many lives were saved. In the collision Captain Sharp lost the testimonials and illuminated address presented to him in recognition of his bravery on the *Paris* in 1890, as well as all his navigational instruments and clothing.

The non-arrival of the SS *Seaford* at Newhaven caused much concern until the *Lyons*, thanks to the good seamanship of Captain Gauvin, arrived safely in the harbour at 8p.m., towing two boats. The injured passengers were taken to hospital, but Charles Pickard decided to return to Dieppe that evening on the night sailing. Captain Lambert, the marine superintendent, and Mr Reeves, railway superintendent, organised special trains for those passengers who wished to carry on with their journeys. The *Lyons* was examined and found to be more seriously damaged than first thought. The passengers were so impressed with the way Richard Sharp and his crew handled the situation that they organised a collection to help compensate them for the loss of their personal possessions. One of the donations came from a Captain Perchel who had read of the sinking in an English newspaper in Italy in which the stokers in the engine room were reported to have made sure there was no danger of an explosion before the vessel sank. He was so impressed that it was he who first suggested that a fund should be organised and this was set up at Lewes Old Bank. On 2 December the crews of both the SS *Seaford* and the *Lyons* were presented to the Mayor and Mayoress. In recognition of their efforts the two masters were presented with silver smoker's companions, the two chief officers received a large marble clock each, and other members of the crew received gifts, all engraved with the inscription, 'Souvenir of Public Esteem Seaford and Lyons 21 August 1895'. Forty-two other crew members received sums of money.

An inquiry into the loss of the SS *Seaford* was held that September and it was decided not to proceed with an investigation as enquiries through the Foreign Office to trace the necessary witnesses from the *Lyons* proved unsuccessful. The loss of SS *Seaford* cost

SS *Seaford* in Dieppe, just two days before she collided with the *Lyons*. (By kind permission of Newhaven Maritime Museum)

Passengers transferring from SS *Seaford* onto the *Lyons* before being taken to Newhaven. (By kind permission of Seaford Museum and Heritage Society)

the company a total of £60,000 and it seems a rather ironic twist that she should be wrecked so near to the place whose name she bore.

The last woman to leave the SS *Seaford* was a stewardess called Isobel Woodall who was born at nearby Bishopstone in the late 1850s. She trained to be a midwife at Queen Charlotte's Hospital in London, and after the SS *Seaford* disaster joined the Union Castle Shipping Company. Many years after her death, a relative presented Seaford Museum with two of her most treasured possessions – oil paintings of the ship.

Divers David Ronnan and Sylvia Pryer, who run the charter business Dive 125 using the boat *Our W*, recovered a plate containing the London, Brighton & South Coast Railway logo, which is now the property of the Bluebell Railway Museum, after they offered a salvage award via the receiver of wrecks.

There have been many shipping casualties along the South Coast, but the stranding of the biggest sailing ship in the world has an unusual story. The *Preussen*, named after the state and kingdom of Prussia, was a fine steel-hulled German ship, the only one of her class with five masts and carrying six sails. On Monday 31 October 1910, she left Hamburg carrying a general cargo, including pianos, for Valparaiso in Chile, a journey she had done on twelve previous occasions, as well as a voyage around the world via New York and Yokohama in Japan. The tug, *President Leeuw*, towed her down the river Elbe and to the North Sea and into the Channel, passing the Royal Sovereign light around 9.50p.m. on 5 November. As there was a fresh north-north-west wind blowing the tug was discharged, and all sails were set by 11.45p.m.

Photograph of the London, Brighton
& South Coast Railway Company
logo, on a plate recovered by divers.
(By kind permission of David Ronnan
and Sylvia Pryer)

The wind abated, but the *Preussen* only made slow headway by 4 knots and with the weather being so hazy the captain gave the order for fog signals to be sounded. A little before midnight he spotted two masthead lights and very soon after the red sidelight of the Newhaven–Dieppe steamer *Brighton* with around ninety passengers on board, about 2 miles to starboard. Her master, Captain Hemmings, saw the *Preussen*'s green light on his port bow and tried unsuccessfully to pass under the *Preussen*'s bow. Captain Nissen on the *Preussen* immediately put his ship's head hard to starboard and ran the starboard engine at full stern, whilst giving a short blast on the whistle, but a collision could not be avoided. The bowsprit of the *Preussen* took out the mainmast and fore funnel of the *Brighton*, causing considerable damage to her port side, whilst the *Preussen* sustained a hole around 15ft below the waterline. After the collision the *Brighton* turned around and came close to the *Preussen* so that the captains could exchange names, and asked if they needed assistance. Both refused, although the *Preussen*'s captain did ask for a tug, and at Newhaven the *Alert* was duly summoned.

Meanwhile, Captain Nissen decided it was impossible to proceed, as the sails and principal parts of the rigging were damaged, and on Sunday morning the masts were cleared as best they could. The captain then decided to take the ship into Dover harbour for temporary repairs and, although at 10a.m. the Meteorological Office issued a gale warning, Captain Nissen did not consider they were in any danger and steered the ship eastward.

He reached Dungeness assisted by three tugs, the *Alert*, the Belgian *John Bull* and the German *Albatross*, and anchored in East Bay. He asked the crew to carry out some temporary repairs so that he could sail back to Hamburg. If it didn't work, he had the option to sail to Dover as the tugs stood by. Around 2.30p.m. on 6 November the *Preussen* went into a wind and her starboard anchor was dropped. The winds reached gale force and she lost her anchors and cables forcing Captain Nissen to ask the three tugs to take him into Dover with a Trinity House pilot, Mr Dixon, on board. All sails furled, tow ropes were attached to the *John Bull* and starboard bow, the *Albatross* to the port side, and the *Alert* made fast on the starboard side. The vessels set off for the eastern side of the harbour, but as they drew close a very strong gust of wind came up and the three tugs could not keep such a heavy ship in position and the tow rope attached to the *John Bull* parted. Captain Nissen realised the only way to save his ship was by using his sails, so the hawsers of the other two ships were slipped and the *Preussen's* crew set her topsails. The yards of the three masts to aft were braced aback while the sails of the fore and main masts were kept shivering, so that she wouldn't be driven too much to the leeward side. The crew did their best and distance from the shore slowly increased, and they thought they were out of imminent danger, but then the forward part of the vessel touched a submerged rock and she was driven broadside towards the shore. By 4.30p.m. she was stranded, and because of the high tides it was impossible for the tugs to make her fast again. She was bumping heavily on the rocks and by 8p.m. had taken 50cm of water into her hold. The coastguards at St Margaret's and at East Cliff were alerted and the lifeboat kept at the top of the Stone Apron was made ready for launching. The lifebelts were brought from the boathouse near the Clock Tower, and the lifeboat launched into a violent south-south-west gale. The lifeboat battled its way to the *Preussen*, whilst the East Cliff coastguards took the rocket apparatus along the cliff top on a cart. The cliff above Fan Bay has a deep drop, so it was decided to lower the rocket apparatus onto the foreshore. Coastguard Arthur Hughes secured a basket-work helmet to his head to protect him from falling stones and climbed down the cliff. The rocket was fired from the foreshore landing on the *Preussen* between the second and third masts. A green light shone from the lifeboat onto the sea side of the wreck, and Coxswain Brockman got close enough to call to the crew on board, but they and two passengers, one the artist and photographer Grad Larsich, refused to abandon ship as they still believed she could be refloated. The lifeboat returned to her station towed by a tug, and after several hours beneath the cliffs, Arthur Hughes returned to the top of the cliffs where he informed his chief officer that he had established a line, but was uncertain if the crew were still on board. Later that evening distress signals again were seen coming from the *Preussen* and the lifeboat launched for a second time. The sea was even heavier, so it was forced to stand off the stranded ship for several hours until eventually able to approach her. Yet again, the crew refused to leave and so the lifeboat returned to her station, arriving back at 5a.m. in the morning. For the third time it was launched and stood by as efforts were made to refloat the *Preussen* on the high tide. A number of tugs – some say up to

Model of the *Preussen* in a bottle at Newhaven Museum. (Conrad Hughes, by kind permission of Newhaven Maritime Museum)

twelve – assembled off Fan Bay, as huge sea waves repeatedly swept over the stranded ship. The lifeboat crew could see between forty and fifty men huddled together near the amidships deck-house, and all appeared to be wearing lifebelts as they waved hats at the gathering crowd. The tugs manoeuvred for over an hour but none came close enough to be able to get a line aboard the stranded ship, and were forced to abandon the rescue. Captain Nissen came ashore to talk with those who were trying to save his ship and gave a statement to the press:

> I was to Valparaiso with a crew of forty-eight and two passengers – one a painter of landscapes, the other a navigating instructor. I had a general cargo of 5000 tons. Off Newhaven I had let go my tug and was making sail when I sighted the *Brighton*. I thought she was going astern, but somehow we collided. Afterwards three tugs picked me (the *Preussen*) up, for I was too damaged to go on, but at Dover, owing to the gale and the sea, the cables broke, and we went ashore. I am proud of my men. When the lifeboats came to us they said to me, 'Captain, we will stick by you. At the worst we can swim ashore, and we have lifebelts.' They were cheerful, and they sang the night through at the pumps as they worked. They did not mind, and we were fairly comfortable, although she lifted and bumped heavily, but not much sea came aboard, for my ship is high. Even the passengers did not mind, and when I came off they decided to remain on the ship. They are brave fellows. I want to be back with them tonight, but no boat can put me aboard. Tomorrow I go back and I hope then to get my ship off and to have her pumped clear.'

On Tuesday morning the two passengers came ashore and later that day eighteen of the younger crew members were brought ashore and taken to a Sailors' Home. Before they abandoned ship the captain mustered the crew on deck and read a telegram that had been received from the Kaiser by the owners of the ship. It read:

> Deeply moved by the news of the disaster to the proud five-masted *Preussen*. I desire to express to the owners my warmest sympathy. I should like a direct report regarding the result of the catastrophe and especially about the fate of the brave crew, which causes me anxiety.

The captain called for three cheers for the Emperor, and after some of the crew had left, the remainder set about lifting pumping gear on board from the *Albatross* and, although during that night the *Albatross* came alongside and tried to reduce the water, it continued to flow in and then out the other side through the large holes in her hull. It was obvious the ship could not be saved, and arrangements were made with the North German Salvage Company, who owned the *Albatross*, to deal with her cargo. Crowds of spectators gathered on the shore commenting on the fact that despite the weather the crew were slow to bring the cargo ashore. Eventually everyone came ashore in lifeboats, and later the vessel broke into two. The Sea Court Inquiry acknowledged the bravery of coastguard Arthur Hughes, who climbed down the cliffs in difficult conditions, and it

The *Preussen* in full sail.
(By kind permission of
Seaford Museum and
Heritage Society)

The *Preussen*, her sail
gone and drifting. (By
kind permission of
Seaford Museum and
Heritage Society)

A further view of
the *Preussen* drifting
towards Dover. (By
kind permission of
Newhaven Maritime
Society)

The *Brighton*, with her mainmast and fore-funnel taken out when she collided with the *Preussen*. (By kind permission of Newhaven Maritime Museum)

Daily Mirror newspaper headline from March 1912 showing the rescued passengers from the P&O liner *Oceana*. (By kind permission of Newhaven Maritime Museum)

The Daily Mirror

THE MORNING JOURNAL WITH THE SECOND LARGEST NET SALE.

No. 2,620.   MONDAY, MARCH 18, 1912   One Halfpenny.

THRILLING RESCUE OF MORE THAN 200 PEOPLE AT DAWN AFTER COLLISION BETWEEN P. & O. LINER AND GERMAN BARQUE IN THE CHANNEL.

The *Pisagua* making her way to Dover for repairs. (By kind permission of Newhaven Museum)

was claimed he was awarded a gold watch by the German Kaiser for his gallant attempt to get a lifeline aboard the wreck of the *Preussen*. The findings did not attach any blame on Captain Nissen for the collision or the stranding of the ship, in fact they entrusted him with command of the newly built *Peking*, which he captained for many years until after the First World War.

Now a hundred years after the event reading through information about that night in November 1910, some interesting facts are coming to light. I have tried to give as accurate an account as possible of what really happened that night, but it is hard to separate fact from fiction. Local rumour states that on the night before sailing Captain Hemmings of the *Brighton* and the tug's skipper Pasco had been enjoying the Lewes Bonfire Celebrations and were 'legless' when they returned. This delayed the ship's departure and later, in the 1930s, the port watchman described them as supporting each other, staggering along the quay in good spirits, but there are also discrepancies over time, speed etc., and Pascoe, who went out to help with the salvage, was described by the Judge at the compensation case 'as the most convincing liar he had ever met' and Pascoe boasted proudly of it for years to come. What really happened that night may be a mystery, but we do know that aboard the *Preussen* were china, glassware, candlesticks, furniture, and possibly a hundred grand pianos, many of which were taken off the wreck and apparently sold in Dover.

Another ship belonging to the same owners as the *Preussen*, the *Pisagua*, was in collision with the P&O liner *Oceana* and the story made national headlines after she struck the liner at right angles, tearing two large holes in her hull. The *Oceana* was en route from London to Bombay with forty passengers and a crew of 210, carrying a mixed cargo of gold and silver bars estimated to be worth around £747,110, together with a large amount of ivory, when she collided and sank on 5 March 1912. The *Pisagua*, a four-masted steel barque, was a famous ocean-racer of the German Laeisz Line. She was in full sail, with the wind behind her, travelling at 20 knots, when she encountered the *Oceana* and assumed that the liner would give way to sail. Unfortunately the *Oceana* didn't see the *Pisagua* soon enough to take evasive action and made the situation worse by turning the wrong way. *Oceana*'s lifeboats were lowered, but became swamped and capsized, drowning nine people, including seven passengers. Those left on board were safely rescued by the cross-Channel steamer *Sussex*, which had picked up a radio distress call. The Newhaven tug *Alert* started to tow the *Oceana* stern first, but she began listing so Captain Hyde and his crew, who had stayed with the ship, were forced to abandon ship and were taken onto the *Alert*. The towing cables were cut, and by Sunday 16 March she sunk off Eastbourne but it took twenty minutes for her to go down. Divers were quick on the scene, taking only ten days to salvage the gold and silver. Ingots with a value of £3,000 were reportedly left behind, and in 1996 a diver found one silver ingot. The *Pisagua* survived the incident and was taken to Dover for repairs.

Seven

WISER AFTER THE EVENT

IN OCTOBER 1853 the *Dalhousie* floundered off Beachy Head, with the loss of sixty men, women and children because, it is alleged, she was top-heavy as the cargo had not been stored properly. This was in the days before Samuel Plimsoll invented his legal loading line. The 800-ton, fully rigged *Dalhousie* was built of Indian teak in 1848, the property of Mr Allen, a ship owner of Leadenhall Street, London and chartered to Fry and Davidson of Fenchurch Street as one of the White Horse Line of Australian passenger ships.

She left the East India Docks at Blackwall on 12 October bound for Sydney, Australia with a general cargo worth £100,000, ten passengers, and a crew of sixty, under the command of Captain Butterworth. He was an experienced captain who was accompanied by his wife and initially three sons, but the eldest went ashore at Deal with the pilot and returned to school in the area. His mother and two brothers remained on the ship and planned to go ashore at Portsmouth, where other passengers were scheduled to join the ship.

The *Dalhousie*'s departure from the Down was telegraphed through to Lloyd's on 18 October and, after leaving around 7a.m. the following morning, she proceeded down the English Channel with a north-west breeze. At about 10a.m. the wind fell off Dungeness, and Captain Butterworth continued slowly under full sail. Between 7p.m. and 9p.m. that night the wind shifted to south-east and gradually freshened. By 10p.m. the watch took in the topsails, and by midnight, with the wind increasing from the south-east, the crew were called to help with the reef topsails. On the starboard bow Beachy Head light was in view and twenty-two-year-old Joseph Reed took the helm. Two hours later the fore and main topsails were reefed and the mizzen topsail stowed away, as it was blowing a gale, accompanied by a heavy sea. Sometime after 4a.m. she began to roll deeply, going over a long way each time, and had difficulty recovering. The

A rare engraving of the *Dalhousie*. (By kind permission of Seaford Museum and Heritage Society)

starboard quarter of the ship was carried away by the sea, and by 5a.m. the crew threw overboard water-casks, sheep-pens and other deck gear in an attempt to right the ship, but it didn't help, and soon after her long boat was carried away. Half an hour later she rolled right over on her starboard beam ends, her mastheads trailing in the water.

Captain Butterworth, four passengers and some of the crew managed to get into the quarter galley on the weather side of the ship, as it was now impossible to stand on the deck. Reed kept a cool head throughout, and together with another seaman rescued a young lady trapped in one of the cabins and brought her into the galley, but heavy seas rushed though the galley and swept four passengers into the sea.

It soon became evident the vessel could not remain afloat much longer, and Captain Butterworth, the second mate and two seamen quitted the galley on a spar. Many people by this time had drowned, but others held onto the weather side of the wreck. Reed, the cook and the carpenter were now the only persons in the quarter galley. Ten minutes after Captain Butterworth left the *Dalhousie*, she slipped under and sank. Reed scrambled out of the quarter deck into the mizzen rigging, and managed to hang on to a piece of timber all morning and most of the afternoon, and watched several vessels pass near, one within only 100 yards, without seeing him.

It was not until 4p.m. that afternoon that the *Dalhousie* was finally sighted and rescued by the brig *Mitchel Grove*, travelling from Littlehampton to Sunderland. It anchored off Dover and sent a boat ashore to report the total loss of the *Dalhousie* and brought ashore her sole survivor, Joseph Reed, who had only been a short time in Mr Allen's service. He had clung to a piece of the wreck, the chock, a piece of timber which supports the

The fine wool clipper *Coonatto* battling her way through the strong sea. (By kind permission of Newhaven Museum)

long boat on the deck, and was washed off it at least twelve times. During the next week large quantities of wreckage were washed up between Hastings and Rye and the body of one of the passengers, a Mrs Underwood, cast up on the beach at Dymchurch. Ironically the life of a Miss Hills was saved because on Friday 14 October she was off Gravesend in a boat hoping to board the *Dalhousie*, but the captain refused to stop. However the Underwood family were not so lucky. Mr Underwood, his wife and two children were also following the *Dalhousie*, and employed a tug to overtake the ship so they could board. He and his family were dragged through the galley window and perished when the sea swept them off the wreck.

In 1982 a Newhaven fisherman's nets snagged leading to work being carried out on the site by a Jersey-based salvage company. They recovered pintles (a pin or bolt used as a vertical pivot or hinge on a rudder) from the rudder of the *Dalhousie*, a section of the hull, mast bands, and other items. Later recoveries have included part of the ship's wheel and the compass housing.

Just below the Seven Sisters cliffs, about 2 miles west of Beachy Head, sits the broken wooden ribs and planking of the port side of the *Coonatto*. She was a fine wool clipper and is important historically because she was built at a time of transition: when the construction of hulls of large ships was changing from wood to iron, and the method of power was changing from sail and wind to engine. She was the smallest rigged ship using John Jordan's revolutionary new construction involving a metal-framed hull supported

Engraving of the *Coonatto* being driven ashore with the Newhaven lifeboat to the foreground. (By kind permission of Seaford Museum and Heritage Society)

by an outer planking skin, making the *Coonatto* both iron- and timber-framed, but still powered by sail. Like all clippers of the time she was built for speed and resembled the famous *Cutty Sark* in appearance. This was the age of great competition between greedy ship owners, moody masters and murderous mates who ruled the seas, and in order to gain more profit, the Samuel Plimsoll line rule had not been observed and the *Coonatto* was overloaded. She was built in London at the shipyard of Thomas Bilbe in 1863, and since she traded with Australia she was named after Coonatto, a township in Australia, which changed its name in 1941 to Moochbra. During her thirteen-year service she was captained by three men: the notorious Captain 'Beastie' Begg and his murderous mate Bad Boy Brennan, who was accused of putting a cabin boy in the stew; Captain Smart; and finally Captain Hillman, who managed to wreck two ships in his short life. At the time of the wrecking he was thirty-one years old, a Londoner who obtained his master's certificate in 1868. *Coonatto* was capable of making the journey in three months, compared to the six to nine months that was the usual voyage time for older East Indiamen, and part of the reason for the speed was the bow, shaped to cut through the water unlike the rounded bows of the slower earlier ships.

At the time of the disaster, the *Coonatto*, owned by the Orient Line, began her last voyage in Adelaide on 14 November 1875, carrying a cargo of bales of wool and copper ingots. She passed the Lizard of Cornwall around 2.30p.m. on the afternoon of 19 February 1876, and made her way up the English Channel, but by 4.15a.m. in the

A copper and ore ingot recovered from the *Coonatto* and now on display at Newhaven Museum. (Conrad Hughes, by kind permission of Newhaven Maritime Museum)

early hours of 21 February she ran into a storm and thick fog off Beachy Head and found herself on the rocks at Crowlink, just west of the Belle Tout lighthouse. The local Lloyd's agent requested the tugs *Victoria* and *Orleans*, and the Newhaven lifeboat *Elizabeth Boys* to offer assistance. The lifeboat made its way to the *Coonatto* and stood by in case it was needed, but by 3p.m. she returned to Newhaven, as the crew on the *Coonatto* were instructed to come ashore, but as far as we can determine her crew were lost, including her captain Beastie Begg and his mate Bad Boy Brennan. Now with the vessel under the control of the agents, the crew returned to London by train and salvage work started immediately, continuing until most of the cargo was recovered. By Saturday night a gale blew up turning the *Coonatto* broadside to the sea, and she broke up on the rocks, with her iron framework and pieces of teak scattered among the chalk boulders of the shoreline at the foot of the Seven Sisters cliffs.

The reason for her loss was claimed to be a navigational error by her captain as he sailed her into a gathering storm, estimated to be 19 knots. The jib snapped under the enormous pressure and as a direct result the topmasts were carried away. She drifted helplessly, stern first, through the gale until she came ashore under the cliffs. Later, because of his error, Hillman's certificate was suspended for three months, and at the time of the wreck there was talk even that the *Coonatto* had been wrecked deliberately for the insurance money, but this has never been proven. It was reported that the ship's figurehead 'sailor lass' stood for many years by a pond at East Dean as a reminder of that fateful day, and was last heard of in Florida, USA. Copper ingots and other artefacts from the *Coonatto* can be seen today at Newhaven Local and Maritime Museum. Hillman eventually returned to sea as captain of the *Inch Kenneth*, but that ship foundered in October 1877, and he drowned.

Sometimes even the best laid plans can go wrong. The *Sussex Daily News* reported that Dr Charles Cunningham, of Eastbourne, loved racing yachts, and had arranged a sailing race between his newly acquired schooner yacht the *Vestal* and the Queensland government's iron ship *Northern Monarch*. Having previously enjoyed many successes in competitions with his yacht *Maria*, he was looking forward to another challenging race.

The *Vestal* had been lying neglected for many years in the mud on the banks of the River Adur at Shoreham-by-Sea when Dr Cunningham purchased her, and although she had not been built as a racer, he was confident he could restore the fast cruising yacht to her former glory. These vessels were built with a flat bottom, a deep keel, and a sharp bow and long quarter. He appointed Stow and Stow at Lower Road in Shoreham-by-Sea to rig and refit her so that she could enter the non-stop race from Plymouth to Brisbane, Australia. The race was set to take place on Saturday 24 November 1883 and expected to take ninety days, arriving in Australia in February 1884.

James Glazebrook, of Eastbourne, was appointed captain, with his son Bristowe and two boys making up the crew. All four helped to load some food needed for the voyage, the rest to be picked up at Plymouth. The race should have begun on the Saturday from Plymouth, but unfortunately due to a neap (shallow) tide the *Vestal* could not sail. Weather permitting, it was hoped the tide would lift her, but due to a mistake she was delayed and would sail on the high tide early on Monday morning. On Sunday night the captain, his son and the two boys went on board at around nine in the evening. The vessel was properly moored and shored on either side to prevent her from listing, as outside a gale was blowing. Those on board could feel the vessel vibrating in the wind, but took no notice. A full-scale thunderstorm was taking place and the winds ripped though the rigging, but as the vessel rested on firm ground the crew were not worried. At around 5a.m. on Monday the captain noticed that the wind had died down but then a sudden flash of lightning lit up the cabin and a sudden gust of wind took the legs holding up the leeward side of the vessel, throwing the *Vestal* completely over on her starboard side. The captain's berth was on the lee side of the vessel and he felt a jerk but thought nothing of it. His son, sleeping on the weather side, was thrown from his berth, over a table and onto a bunk on the opposite side of the cabin. One of the boys was also thrown across the vessel and landed in another berth. Luckily they were not injured, but the crew were in complete darkness and had no way of communicating with each other. All exit avenues from the cabins were tightly jammed, making it difficult to get from one part of the yacht to another but eventually all four escaped through the skylight. All were undressed as everything had been thrown around their cabins, and, without lights, they could not find their clothes, but the four cold half-naked seamen found temporary shelter in the nearest public house. The crew were unable to save any of their processions, and an examination of the wreck later revealed that she was full of water. When the tide receded the *Vestal* was a total wreck, having keeled over with such force that the part below the water where the sides curve inwards had been staved in, breaking her ribs and planks like matchwood. The cabin floor had broken up, the beams overhead snapped in two and the bow was split, allowing water to flow into the vessel, as well as through the bottom. The *Vestal* was not alone as, during this storm, many of the vessels moored in the harbour filled with water and sank too. Meanwhile

the *Northern Monarch* was left to begin her voyage alone, and the Australian *Hawera &
Normaby Star* newspaper to report the loss of the *Vestal* on 28 November.

The stubbornness of the captain on the British collier *Arno* must have caused much
distress to those trying to help her. She left Sunderland on Thursday 9 February 1899
bound for Portsmouth with a crew of seventeen, as well as 1,300 tons of coal destined
for the gasworks. Two days later she was heading towards Spithead and although there
was a gale and rough seas, Captain Stansfield felt confident, as he knew the waters well,
but his self-assurance may have lead to a series of mistakes that contributed to the *Arno's*
demise. By 7.20p.m. that evening they were level with the Owers Lightship, 8 miles
south of Selsey Bill, in waters renowned for dangerous sandbanks, but the captain set
a course a little to the north-west before going below to find some warmer clothing.
Returning twenty minutes later, he discovered the ship had drifted to the north, and
ordered a change of course three degrees to the left, but he did not check his position,
which would normally involve taking bearings of any surrounding buoys or aids.

By this time the weather worsened and a large wave hit the bridge, smashing windows
and putting out the compass light and, after another wave around 8.30p.m., the ship hit
a sandbank. Captain Stansfield had made the mistake of not taking into account the
strong east-north-east current, helped by the gale, which had pushed the *Arno* into the
path of danger. He steered to the left, managing to get the ship afloat again, and ordered
the carpenter to inspect the bottom for damage. He returned and assured the captain
there was no water seeping in, so Stansfield ordered full steam ahead.

Soon after she was aground again, this time amidships. A crew member reported
that the rear boiler was filling and fearing pressure would build up inside and burst,
Stansfield had its caps released and started to pump out. When the situation became
uncontrollable he ordered the crew to fire distress rockets, which were seen by the
Selsey lifeboat house, who fired the maroon to alert the crew. Meanwhile the distress
signal had also been picked up by two coastguard stations at Bracklesham Bay who also
responded, and just over half an hour later the crew and helpers arrived. The RNLI
lifeboat was launched and about a mile from the *Arno* the lifeboat crew saw her steam
away in the opposite direction. Despite the darkness and the storm they searched for the
ship for many hours, until in the early hours of the morning, but returned without her.

In fact, about a quarter on an hour after the *Arno* had signalled for help, Captain
Stansfield made yet another mistake by thinking the rockets and guns returning his
signal came from a lightship or the shore, and it did not occur to him that they were
reassuring him help was on its way. He was more concerned with the fate of the ship,
and ordered the first mate to prepare the left lifeboat, whilst the second mate dealt with
the right one, but by now the jolly boat, mounted at the rear of the deck, had been
washed overboard. Undeterred Captain Stansfield called the boats in and distributed
lifebelts to his crew, and even personally strapped a few in. At 9p.m. the *Arno* went
aground for the third time, this time heavily at the front. The strong waves lifted her up
and down and she bumped the bottom. Once again water seeped in and also came into

THE YACHT VESTAL.

LONDON, November 27.
The yacht Vestal, which was being
fitted at Shoreham, overturned and filled
with water. The proposed race to Australia between the Vestal, and ship Northern Monarch, will therefore not take
place.

the engine room. With the steam pumps turned on, Stansfield ordered his engineer to carry on until it was no longer safe, hoping that they would find calmer waters. More flares were fired from the rockets, continuing for another two hours, until they found shelter off the Isle of Wight. Water was coming into the stokehole and the engineer reported it lapping against the engine. Finally, as the water put the fire out and the engine stopped, the captain could see no point in carrying on and ordered everyone below deck to come up. Ten minutes later the ship nosedived and Captain Stansfield was thrown into the sea. The first to get into the vessel's lifeboats were Boatswain Thomas Pottinger and Donkeyman William Johnson, but, still tied to the *Arno*, they felt the boat pulling under as the ship began to sink. Thinking quickly they cut the rope just in time but this was not the end of their ordeal and, hearing the cries of fellow shipmates, they rowed upwind hoping to pick them up. They soon discovered that the boat was letting in water, covering the floor, but they did manage to pick up the captain, who was swimming towards the lightship, and then Able Seaman Charles Ryan who was floating on a hatch cover.

Meanwhile the cruiser HMS *Gladiator* had been a mile or so behind the *Arno* and saw her signals. She lowered her lifeboat, sweeping the waves with her searchlight beam, and found the mast-tops of the *Arno* protruding above the water, but despite searching for almost two hours could locate no one else. The four survivors continued downwind and eventually saw the lights of a large town in front of them, and assumed it was Portsmouth as, in the dark, they could make out a large gap which must have been the harbour entrance. The tide was taking them towards the gap, but the gale was pushing them to the side, so they rowed harder in an attempt to stay on course, and soon recognised the Horse Sand Fort, and knew the harbour could not be more than 3 miles away. Passing the fort they shouted, but no one replied. Later the searchlight of the *Gladiator* fell on them, and they thought their ordeal was again over, but amazingly the men on the warship did not see them either. The tug *Camel* came out of the harbour to join in the search and was on course to meet the lifeboat, but yet again the crew did not see the shipwrecked sailors who were forced to take evasive action to get out of the way. Even the Southsea lifeboat passed close by and the survivors could not attract attention. Finally, four hours after their ship sank the four approached the sea wall of

The *Miown* sinking fast as Captain Jones waits to be rescued. (By kind permission of West Sussex County Council Library Service)

Southsea Castle, exhausted and powerless to stop the craft from being pushed towards the piles that guarded the castle wall. As the boat was lifted and smashed against the piles, they managed to muster the last of their strength to jump clear. Pottinger and Stansfield managed to climb to the top of the wall and trudged along Granada Road, where they found Police Constable Cordroy. After explaining their story, Cordroy and some soldiers went in search of Johnson and Ryan. Johnson had broken his leg trying to scale the wall and was still clinging on when found. Ryan had managed to reach the top, and was found by a master gunner before fainting. The gunner administered artificial respiration and took him into the castle. Sadly the remaining thirteen drowned, and in due course six of the bodies were washed ashore at Bracklesham Bay. It transpired that Captain Stansfield, who had only held his master's certificate for three and a half years, claimed that the *Arno* sank just north-west of the (then) Nab Lightship in 15 fathoms of water – some 4½ miles from the entrance of Chichester harbour. Battered by the sea, there is little of the *Arno* left now, but her boilers stand proud at the bottom of the sea.

There is a seafaring superstition that it is unlucky for a ship to set sail on the thirteenth of the month, and although the *Miown* didn't actually sail on that day, it seems the unlucky number thirteen may have had a hand in her fate. The small British steamship *Miown* left London for Bristol on 12 February 1914 under the command of Captain Walter Jones and a crew of eight, carrying a cargo of cement. The *Miown* ran into a gale, so Captain Jones decided to make for the shelter of the Isle of Wight, but by midnight on 13 February, in the grips of a south-east gale and being battered by the sea, he decided to change course and make for the safety of Shoreham harbour instead. For some unknown reason *Miown* was too close to the shore at Shoreham and at 2a.m. Captain Jones ordered a course towards the harbour lights. Just 1½ miles from the harbour she struck a low reef and sank so quickly that no distress signals were sent out and the crew only had time to think of saving themselves. The captain urged the men to stay with the ship as he climbed the rope ladder to the mast but they took no notice. Four of the crew started to launch the ship's lifeboat, but were swept overboard. The ship's mate begged two more crew members to jump and swim to safety, and all three plunged into the cold seawater, and were not seen again. Now with water sweeping the decks the engineer was forced to climb the mainmast where the captain was still clinging on. Later the captain noticed something swinging and hitting the stays of the mast that was in danger of pulling them both into the sea, so he clambered down and cut it free with his knife, but the structure that kept them clear of the waves was less safe. All through that night the two men clung to the swaying mast with only the lights of the harbour in the distance to keep their spirits up. When dawn broke the captain found he was alone, having been exposed to the elements for nearly six hours, and he prayed that someone somewhere would have noticed him. Unknown to him, during the night, the masthead light on the *Miown* had been spotted, but it was assumed all was well and the ship had anchored, waiting for the incoming tide before coming into harbour. Luckily for Captain Jones someone decided to take a closer look.

John Short, a waterman living in one of the cottages facing the sea at Southwick, awoke at dawn and saw the masthead lights. Using his field glasses he saw that there were three masts and a funnel sticking out of the water with a figure of a man clinging

A bronze cogwheel and brass cap from the steamship *Miown* that sank in Shoreham harbour in 1914. (Conrad Hughes, by kind permission of Marlipins Museum, Shoreham-by-Sea)

The *Comtesse de Flandre*, whose cargo of liquorice kept local boys away from school in 1925. (By kind permission of Seaford Museum and Heritage Society)

The *Comtesse de Flandre* ashore at Seaford. (By kind permission of Seaford Museum and Heritage Society)

to the top mast. He ran to three neighbours, one of whom owned a dingy, and they launched it into the water but, out of the harbour, they were faced with the full force of the gale with waves crashing over the small vessel.

Meanwhile Captain Jones was about to give up all hope when he caught a glimpse of the dingy, and immediately gathered strength to wave his handkerchief to attract attention. After much struggling the three men manoeuvred the dingy into a safe position beneath where the captain was stranded, and at the right moment he slid into it. Another boat was launched by local pilots to search for any survivors amongst the floating wreckage, but there were none. Captain Jones, blue with cold and exhausted, had been rescued in the nick of time and the shivering survivor was wrapped in the rescuers' coats as they made their way back to Southwick Quay. The captain was carried into one of the rescuer's cottages, and placed next to the fire, but he was extremely distressed and kept repeating, 'All hands could have been saved, if only they had stuck with me.' Jones soon recovered and, on the Saturday, returned to his home in Cardiff. Meanwhile telegraph signals were sent to London stating that the tops of the masts were visible from the shore and heavy seas had staved in the hatches, and the Salvage Association had no hope of recovering the ship or the cargo. By the following day the three masts had not been taken by the storm, but the ship's funnel had been washed away. The *Miown*, known as the 'cement wreck', became a danger to shipping, lying slightly to the west of the harbour entrance, and to ensure safe entry to the harbour she was blown apart, but local divers now report that slowly she is emerging from the seabed. The wreck has been declared a voluntary marine reserve, and is usually buoyed during the summer months for safety. A number of her artefacts can be seen at Shoreham Museum.

Finally, in 1925 another ship, the *Comtesse de Flandre*, came to grief under the cliffs near Seaford, but thankfully everyone on board, passengers and crew, were rescued by breeches buoy from the cliff top. The incident was well covered in the national press, but she will be always be remembered, especially by the then children of Seaford who were obviously wiser after the event. The vessel was carrying a cargo of half-processed liquorice, and word soon went around the classrooms that 'sweeties' were scattered all along the shore. The children could hardly wait for the final bell and as soon as the school day was over dashed down to the beach. One had 'borrowed' his neighbour's old penny-farthing and rushed off having no idea how to stop the cycle so he grabbed a branch, hung there and watched the bicycle travel on and crash. Once on the beach, the boys stuffed themselves full of the liquorice. The next day it was reported that few of the boys were in school and, those that did attend, spent most of their time queuing for the lavatory in the playground!

Eight

ILL-FATED SHIPS AND VICTIMS OF TWO WORLD WARS

THE SHIPS in this chapter are here because they were destined to become wrecked along our shores by simply being unlucky or victims of the First and Second World Wars, so we could say they were all in the wrong place at the wrong time. To include all the ships that went down during both world wars would require another book to themselves. So I have selected just a few of many, but the first ship in this chapter is the ill-fated *Henry*.

On the morning of 15 February 1812 the British sailing vessel, *Henry*, on a voyage from Southampton to the north-east of England with a cargo of timber, came up against a French privateer and was chased up the Channel. By 10p.m. that evening she was driven ashore near Beachy Head, and her master, Abraham Reay, simply walked off his ship, leaving his crew on board.

The following morning, John Hayter, an employee on Birling Farm, was told of the stricken ship and asked his informant to alert Mr West and Mr Marsh, the customs officers. Meanwhile Hayter hurried to the wreck and found the master-less crew safe and well but they told him that their master had just marched off and was last seen walking along the beach towards Eastbourne. After discussing how best to salvage what they could, the crew decided to take down the sails, rigging and cables before the tide returned and Hayter told one of the crew, Henry Miller, to go to Birling Farm and bring a team of horses to help with the removal of the salvaged items. Hayter then set off to find the master, and eventually found him fast asleep on the bench in the tap-room of the New Inn, shook him awake and asked if he wanted him to find more hands to help with the salvage operation. Reay was furious and refused help saying the vessel was aground and the incoming tide would soon engulf it and smash her to pieces. The landlady, Mrs Comber, overheard the conversation and suggested that Reay was unwell, and surely could not mean what he said. Now more alert, Reay sat up and

The *Lamburn*, lying on her side ashore at Hastings in 1866. (Michael Myers, by kind permission of David Renno)

Hayter explained more clearly that a team of horses were on their way to help with the salvage, and estimated that at least three wagon-loads could be rescued before the incoming tide. The master was most indignant and told Hayter not to touch a thing on his vessel, but Hayter pointed out that the horses would arrive at the wreck well before he had time to return, but the master was adamant. Hayter quickly returned to the *Henry* and found the crew salvaging what they could, but when he told them what their master had said, they stopped work immediately, unloaded the horses and ordered their return. It was not long before the vessel was smashed to pieces by the incoming tide.

Later Mr Reay made a complaint about Hayter's conduct to W.B. Langridge, a local solicitor, but the content of the complaint was never made public. There had always been problems with access to the shore, the only road being over land belonging to Birling Farm. The owner at the time, Mr Hudson, always kept the gate locked in order to maintain his right and to keep trespassers out. Although always willing to unlock the gates providing he was given a good reason, it is not known whether, with the absence of written documentation, Hayter's intensions were entirely honourable.

Some fifty years later a severe gale caused the wreck of the ill-fated *Lamburn*, a collier brigantine owned by Messrs Kent, who stood to lose a great deal of money with its loss. It seems this thirty-year-old British sailing brig, built in Hastings and launched on 12 February 1833, was doomed from the start by a string of bad luck.

During the evening of 17 November 1866, she came ashore at Hastings. She had been carrying a cargo of coal destined for the Hastings Gas Company but had successfully

The *Gamecock* ashore at Seaford. (By kind permission of Seaford Museum and Heritage Society)

unloaded it and anchored broadside on overnight. The crew settled down for the night but unfortunately a southerly gale blew up and as the winds and waves increased on the rising tide the vessel found herself in danger as only a small anchor held the hauling-off rope. However, despite the situation, the crew remained on board until 4a.m., but it then became extremely dangerous to stay any longer and they abandoned ship. By 6a.m. the intensity of the sea striking the *Lamburn* caused serious damage and, after being struck by three successive waves, the vessel began to roll until she rolled right over onto her starboard side and, with constant battering from the sea, broke up and became a total wreck.

Although there was no loss of life it was considered that, because of her age, the *Lamburn* was no longer seaworthy. Despite having been substantially restored five years earlier after lying on shore at Hastings for many months, this was not *Lamburn*'s first maritime incident, as she was involved in a collision off Hartlepool on 28 September 1849 when she ran into the *Elizabeth* of Whitby. On this occasion the master had been asleep below, and the mate in charge had gone below for some refreshments. Fortunately the crew of the *Elizabeth* were rescued by the *Lamburn* and taken into Hartlepool.

Although the next ship, the *Little Dick*, overturned in 1882, it was not an unlucky vessel, although one of its crew members came up against the unlucky number thirteen. The *Little Dick* was a sailing dandy that worked around the Newhaven area. On the evening of Sunday 2 April 1882 Mr Bradford (the master), Charles Stone and Robert Stevens were en route to collect boulders as ballast when a sudden strong gust of wind caught the *Little Dick* by surprise, capsizing her and throwing the crew into the sea. They managed to scramble onto the upturned vessel and were seen by people out walking. George Green, a local fisherman, rushed for one of his boats and, with the help of others, carried it down to the water's edge and, with a crew of four, rowed to the upturned vessel and took the stranded sailors on board. On arrival at Newhaven, Charles Stone revealed that this was the thirteenth time he had been rescued from the jaws of the sea.

Christmas Eve 1888 saw the unfortunate *Mary Davies* smashed to pieces on the shore at Seaford. The small schooner, loaded with Portland stone, was bound for London when the dilemma began around 10p.m. on Sunday 23 December. She developed a serious leak, and her three-man crew, Master Richard Davies, Thomas Francis and a boy, were kept busy throughout the night manning the pumps, but by the early hours of Christmas Eve a south-westerly gale blew up and she began to leak so badly that Davies decided to make for the safety of Newhaven harbour. As they approached the crew were unable to keep the vessel stable because of the water on board, and the *Mary Davies* drifted helplessly in strong winds, past the harbour entrance. By the time she came ashore between the Martello Tower and Seaford Head, word had reached town that a vessel was in distress. A large number of spectators gathered along the sea wall, watching as the crew tied ropes around their bodies and were hauled safely ashore before the Blatchington coastguards arrived. At the time, the fox-hounds were out on the hill above Seaford, and the huntsmen gave the crew the contents of their flasks before they were taken to the nearby hotel. The sailors, described as 'having had a rough

The *Gamecock* resting on the shingle at Seaford. (By kind permission of Newhaven Museum)

Spectators came to see the *Gamecock*. Note the lady in Edwardian dress sitting on the beach in the front of the picture, in an almost picnic-like scene. (By kind permission of Newhaven Museum)

The start of salvage operation on the *Gamecock*. (By kind permission of Seaford Museum and Heritage Society)

time', welcomed this kindness. The sea continued to wash over *Mary Davies*; by 1p.m. the mast was lost, and within an hour she was reduced to matchwood. However, like most wrecks Seaford's community gained; the cargo of stone was put to good use by the builders who already had begun construction of the Surrey Convalescent Home at Blatchington. They purchased the salvaged cargo of Portland Stone and incorporated it into the stairs and landing of the new building. The home was opened in 1891 and provided care facilities until 1966 when it was demolished for the redevelopment of Surrey Road and Jevington Drive.

In 1908 the unlucky steam trawler *Gamecock* was in trouble on the same stretch of water. She had already had one nerve-racking experience in her lifetime whilst trawling in the North Sea Dogger Bank area in 1904, when for some unexplained reason the *Gamecock* became caught in the Russo-Japanese War, which grew out of territorial expansion in East Asia. She was the leader of a fleet of Pickering and Waldanes trawlers from Hull that were working in the Baltic when the small lights of the fleet were mistaken for the enemy, and the Russians opened fire. After this incident the Hull fleet pulled out of the area, but why the *Gamecock* found herself in the vicinity of Seaford in 1908 remains a total mystery. We do know that she was on her way from Hull with a cargo of fish when she ran into a severe gale crossing Seaford Bay and, with the wind and rough seas, her fate was sealed when she ran short of coal and could make no headway and ran aground opposite the old Tide Mills. The Newhaven lifeboat, *Michael Henry*, which recently had been converted to motor, was launched at around 9.20a.m., but due to the changeover she had a reduced crew. She ran into trouble when she collided with a groyne and her engine failed and, unable to restart, she then ran aground, but thankfully with no loss of life. Rockets carrying rescue lines to the stricken vessel were fired from the beach by the coastguards and, once a line was in place, the crew were brought ashore by breeches buoy.

The *Gamecock's* catch of fish remained aboard the trawler, stinking and rotting, until one day the boys from the Tide Mill village decided to attack their rivals, the Seaford town gang, with a bombardment of the rotten fish!

Eventually the *Gamecock* was refloated by Newhaven tugs *Alert* and *Hauler*, but sadly after the vessel was patched up at Newhaven and returned to her own port for repairs, three months later, she set sail for the North Sea and was never seen again.

Both world wars found many ships sunk in Sussex waters, and it would be impossible to mention them all as it is such a large subject. Instead I have picked a few I hope you find interesting, and maybe whet your appetite to learn more.

The British steamship *Jaffa* left Boulogne at noon on 1 February 1918, in ballast, in charge of a pilot bound for Southampton when she was torpedoed in the early hours of the following morning by the German submarine *UB-30*. Prior to leaving, her captain, William Newton, received confidential instructions concerning the route and navigation from the British Naval Authorities. The pilot left the ship at 12.10p.m., and the *Jaffa* continued her voyage under the command of her captain. Just after midnight on

The *Jaffa* was torpedoed on 2 February by a German U-boat.

2 February with the ship at full speed, a sudden and violent explosion occurred on the portside and amidships. A flash of light was seen and a fountain of water cascaded over the bridge. She sank within three minutes, taking ten men with her, but before doing so her starboard lifeboat was put into the water with her captain and twelve of her crew aboard. Shortly afterwards the U-boat surfaced nearby and the captain was asked for the ship's name, cargo and destination, and then submerged again. The lifeboat sailed on and landed safely at Littlehampton, but the ship's papers and confidential documents went down with the vessel.

The *Jaffa*, acquired by Thomas Wilson & Co. Ltd, had been fitted with refrigeration units and, during the early part of the First World War, was in great demand filling her holds with meat on voyages between England and France. In 1917 Thomas Wilson merged with Sir John Reeves Ellerman Bart to become Ellerman's Wilson Line Ltd, and the *Jaffa* found herself contributing to the Expeditionary Force Transport (EFT) as No. E2160 until her loss.

In 1977 divers recovered a dinner plate with the distinctive blue pennant in a white circle, and the words 'Wilson Line', a positive clue to the identity of the wreck, and when her insignia was found intact, the location of the wreck of the *Jaffa* was confirmed. Today she lies on her port side, her four boilers standing proud. She was armed with a 4.7in gun, and although shell cases dated 1918 have been recovered, the gun has not been found and is probably buried in the silt.

Another war victim, the liner *Shirala* left London on Sunday 30 June 1918 and dropped anchor at Higham Bight on the Gravesend side of the Thames to pick up a cargo of ammunition, and a variety of goods and spare parts, as well as a few passengers for the onward journey to India. On the afternoon tide she sailed down the coast to Nore, and dropped anchor before proceeding on the Tuesday morning. The meteological office recorded a perfect day on 2 July, and within 5 miles of Littlehampton, following a zig-zag Admiralty-planned route so that she would not be hit by a U-boat, a muffled explosion was heard beneath the ship's port side, followed by a second on the starboard side. With her side plates torn and engine room flooded, the *Shirala* sunk amidships with the trapped air compressed into the stem and stern supporting the deadweight of the ship. The middle plates cracked further and the decking plates buckled, forcing her into the air and exposing the single propeller, and in this odd position she sank.

During the summer of 1978 the salvage company Metal Recoveries (Newhaven) Ltd, who owned the cargo, used explosives to split open the hull, resulting in thousands of wine bottles being scattered over a wide area. Her four holds, two on each side of the bridge, revealed an assortment of goods: African ivory elephant tusks, cases of wine, crates of Dundee marmalade in stone jars, spares for lorries and Model T cars (including tyres, axles, radiators and engines), binoculars, telescopes and ammunition, and detonating caps by the thousand.

During the First World War German U-boats were particularly active and successful in destroying both naval and merchant vessels, Many lives were lost as well as essential supplies of food, fuel and munitions being severely impaired, with the English Channel being the resting place for more than 750 First World War wrecks. In fact the seabed off Newhaven, Seaford and Beachy Head is littered with so many wrecks that it has become known as the 'Killing Ground', and one of the popular wrecks that is dived today is that of the *City of Brisbane*. The armed merchantman was travelling in ballast from London to Buenos Aires when she was torpedoed by *UB-57* on 13 August 1918. She quickly filled with water with her stern almost submerged. Tugs from nearby Newhaven struggled all day to try and bring her close enough to the shore to

ELLERMAN'S
WILSON LINE
HULL.

JRE

Passenger Services
to
NORWAY, SWEDEN,
DENMARK & BALTIC
—— STATES. ——

SUBJECT TO ALTERATION OR CANCELLATION WITHOUT NOTICE.

Berths are booked and Passengers carried subject to the conditions shown on the Company's Contract Tickets.

JUNE—SEPTEMBER, 1927.

The *Jaffa* was acquired by Thomas Wilson & Co. Ltd and fitted with refrigeration units. During the early part of the Second World War she filled her holds with meat on voyages between England and France. The company later became the Ellerman's Wilson Line and ran passenger services to Norway, Sweden and Denmark, as well as the Baltic Seas.

be beached and repaired, but her struggle ended just after midnight when the crew were taken off and she sank to the seabed. She now lies in sand and shingle, broken in two with her bow section standing some 5m clear of the seabed and listing to port. The wreck is now owned by Metal Recoveries of Newhaven and anyone wishing to dive should seek permission first.

After sinking the *City of Brisbane*, UB-57 headed for home in Zeebrugge, Belgium, and during the journey checked that the horizon was clear, then started to surface. Upon surfacing her captain Johann Lohs opened the hatch to find he was directly beneath a now-flying British airship. A crash dive was ordered, but the airship had already started to drop bombs and, although they escaped sinking, they continued on their journey home after radioing to say they had sunk 15,000 tons of shipping and were returning to base. Nothing more was ever heard and it would seem that it is likely he hit a mine as Johann Lohs' body and some of UB-57's crew were washed up near the River Scheldt about a week later.

The *Moldavia* and her sister ship the *Mongolia* were the first of the famous P&O 'M' series of enormous passenger liners and at the time, the only criticism concerning their design were the number of portholes – over 1,000 in all – which, according to her builder, made her 'perforated' with holes. The *Moldavia* cost £336,170 to build, and she made her first scheduled sailing from London to Sydney via Colombo and Melbourne on 11 December 1903, proving her 12,000hp engine could push her along at a top speed of 18.5 knots. During the First World War she was converted into an armed merchant cruiser and went down on 23 May 1918 after being hit by a single torpedo from the U-boat UB-57. At the time she was being used as a troopship for American soldiers, and fifty-seven on board were killed, fifty-six in the explosion and one during a leg amputation operation on board a rescue ship. These were the only American casualties during the whole trooping operation in which over one million US troops were carried in British ships. The giant wreck now lies off the coast at Littlehampton in extremely deep waters.

The British steamer *Barnhill* was on the last leg of her journey from Halifax, Nova Scotia to London carrying much needed supplies of copper and tinned food. On Wednesday 20 March 1940 the captain, Michael O'Neill, decided to take a chance and sail eastwards. In the moonlight she was seen making her way up the Channel, just 3 miles south-south-west of Beachy Head, by a German Dornier 17, known to the British as 'flying pencils' because they were long and thin and able to dive faster than any other aircraft. They were effective, in fact too effective, because at 10.45p.m. the aircraft dived and discharged a 550lb bomb that hit the stern, and another went down the ship's funnel. No one on board the *Barnhill* saw the aircraft so no defensive action was taken. Within seconds the ship was ablaze, four of the crew killed and eight badly injured, one of whom died in hospital from his injuries. Captain O'Neill was blown from the deck in the impact and ended up out of view under the debris, and his crew assumed he had been killed too.

HMS *Moldavia*, another victim of a torpedo, whilst she was carrying American troops.

On shore the noise of the explosions woke up the residents of Eastbourne who turned out to see the drama unfold. The Eastbourne lifeboat *Jane Holland* came to the rescue and Coxswain Michael Hardy took off twenty-eight survivors. Shortly afterwards, spectators reported they could hear the ship's bell ringing, so the lifeboat returned to investigate and found Captain O'Neill. He had been knocked unconscious by the explosion and, when he recovered, managed to untangle himself from the twisted metal and realised he was alone on the blazing ship. He called for help, but the lifeboat was out of earshot so, despite having a broken arm, a fractured collar bone and five broken ribs, he stumbled over to the bell and gripped the bell rope with his teeth, shaking his head furiously. By the time the lifeboat returned Captain O'Neill had collapsed with exhaustion and pain. The two men who rescued him, Thomas Allchorn and Alec Huggett, were awarded the RNLI bronze medal for gallantry.

The *Barnhill* drifted until finally she ran aground near Langney Point and it took Eastbourne firemen several days to put out the fire. On the third day she broke in two, but the firemen managed to escape before she did so. A month later her cargo began to come ashore, and with wartime rationing still in operation, many a pantry in Eastbourne welcomed the extra bonus of tinned meat, stew and baked beans. All that remains today, to be seen at low tide, are three large rounded 'humps', the ship's metal boilers.

After leaving Newhaven in ballast for Mumbles, near Swansea, the *Frode* was hit by a German parachute mine on 13 April 1943 and sank with the loss of seven of her crew of seventeen; two more men later died in hospital of their injuries. The wreckage came ashore between 13 and 19 April. She was seized on 25 April 1918 and taken to Germany. The *Frode* now lies scattered or buried in only 6m of water. A local fisherman fixed a permanent buoy to the split-open boiler, the largest piece of wreckage. She was badly smashed and even now, items continue to come to light from the seabed. The *Frode*, a

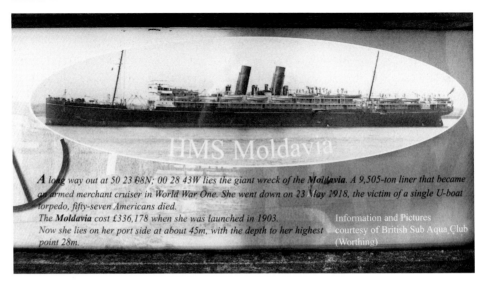

Story board near Worthing Pier relating to the loss of the *Moldavia*. (Conrad Hughes)

A map showing the position of wrecks near to Worthing on a story board near Worthing Pier. (Conrad Hughes)

Close-up of the map showing the location of the *Indiana, Miown, Jaffa, Masslust* and *Moldavia* on a story board near Worthing Pier. (Conrad Hughes)

Norwegian coaster, had a chequered life and was originally owned by a Dutch company based at Rotterdam and called the *Hollandia I*. She was seized on 25 April 1918 by *U-19* and taken to Germany. She returned to her Dutch owners in 1919, and in 1924 was sold on to A/S Garm of Norway and renamed *Frode*. Later, in 1931 she was sold yet again to another Norwegian company, Rederi A/S Steinmann, and in April 1940 was chartered by the Ministry of Shipping in London, who in turn became charterers to the Ministry of War Transport. On 15 January 1941, she was beached at Oban after a fire caused severe damage but was refloated in August, and less than two years later she was wrecked off Newhaven.

The merchant steamship SS *Storaa* was built in 1918 at Greenock and by 1940 was owned by the Hetland Company of Denmark. The Danish registered her under the Red Ensign on 27 May 1940 and under Captain Jens Fage Pedersen she sailed for Bayonne with a cargo of coal, then on to Casablanca in Morocco. At the time French Morocco was under German control and she was captured at Casablanca on 27 July and impounded with other merchant ships at Port Hyailey, now called Kenitra on the Sebou river, about 80 miles north. For two and a quarter years until 10 November 1942, Captain Pedersen and his crew remained in Morocco and he used every means possible to stop the ship from being used by the enemy. On 14 September 1941 *Storaa*'s first mate, Max Mikkelsen, escaped in a stolen lifeboat with another man and sailed to Gibraltar, a distance of some 160 miles, which involved going down the Sebou river, under the French guns in the Arab fort, then north out into the open sea. During this time they lived off eight bottles of claret and twelve tins of sardines. They were recorded in the crew book as 'disappeared', as were all escapees. Once in Britain Max joined the Special Operations Executive (SOE) and parachuted into Denmark as an underground radio operator, until he was caught. In the final days before the Allied invasion *Storaa* was ransacked and sunk at her moorings, but she was seized by the British Ministry of War Transport and Captain Pedersen was instructed to raise her, fit her out and sail her to Newcastle. She arrived at Newcastle on 7 June 1943, armed and made ready for the British Government war service. Captain Pedersen and a British Danish crew prepared for a dangerous Atlantic voyage. On 20 August the *Storaa* sailed from Oban, Scotland in convoy to Sheet harbour near Halifax, Nova Scotia arriving on 1 September, and she departed from Halifax with convoy SC143 on 28 September, being designated a rescue ship on 8 October. The German *U-610* torpedoed the Polish destroyer escort *Orkan* (ex-HMS *Myrmidon*) and sank her with the loss of 178 Polish and twenty British lives. The convoy arrived at Loch Ewe in Scotland on 12 October 1943, and by the time *Storaa* had returned to Britain the Allies were preparing for an invasion of Europe the following year. The British countryside was being stockpiled with tanks, aircraft, barges, guns and ammunition ready for D-Day, with Eisenhower as Commander. The railways were already busy so it was decided that some of the supplies should be sent by sea from the Thames to Cardiff. Sadly this was to be *Storaa*'s final voyage. Wartime records show that *Storaa*'s cargo consisted of tons of steel pylons as well as caterpillar

The *Barnhill* ablaze off Eastbourne on 20 March 1940, with the Newhaven lifeboat attending, displaying her name, despite wartime security, and the naval fire tug attempting to douse the flames aboard. (By kind permission of Newhaven Maritime Museum)

The *Barnhill* aground near Langney Point, near Eastbourne. It took Eastbourne firemen several days to put out the fire.

tracks for tanks and crated aircraft, some of which were stored on the deck. Using merchant ships to carry deck cargo for military purposes were common, and the *Storaa* was loaded in the Thames Estuary under the supervision of the third mate, Hendrik Knudson. Twenty ships left for Cardiff on the night of 2 November 1943, intending to slip unseen passed the German enemy guns along the French coast and avoid the E-boats. However, at 12.30a.m. on 3 November, 10 miles off Hastings, the *Storaa* was hit by a torpedo from E-boat *S-138* under the command of Lieutenant Stohwasser, and sank within 30 seconds. Twenty-one men died, including Captain Jens Pedersen who had done so much to protect his crew and save his ship from enemy use. Only sixteen survived. The Dover pilot Watson Peverley who had guided the convoy through the Dover minefields also died.

Purely by chance, the location of the *Storaa* was found by the Government Archaeological Diving Unit led by Martin Dean of St Andrews University, and confirmed when every detail of the wreck matched the ship.

The galley boy on board the *Storaa* at the time she went down was Bernard Griffiths, born on 11 August 1925 at Knutsford, Cheshire. Together with his sister Agnes and brother, he was taken into care when he was six and moved to a children's home in Liverpool. At the age of thirteen Bernard was transferred to the National Nautical School at Portishead, near Bristol, and became a galley boy on the *Storaa* and was only eighteen when he died in the disaster. His story and that of the *Storaa* can be found at the Shipwreck Museum at Hastings, who have carried out considerable research into this ship.

Royal Naval wrecks are protected as war graves, but there are thousands of merchant navy ships that sank during the two world wars that are not, and in 1985 the Ministry of Defence sold the rights to salvage the wreck to two divers for £150. One of the men who died on SS *Storaa* was Petty Officer James Varndell, a naval gunner, and his daughters argued that, as a war grave, the wreck should be protected from both commercial salvage and leisure divers under the Protection of Military Remains Act. One of the daughters, who was twelve at the time of her father's death, said that although her father was in the Royal Navy, his grave is not recognised because he was on a merchant navy ship. The case went to the High Court in 2005, and the Merchant Navy Association saw it was an important test case in its campaign to have merchant navy wrecks given the same protection as those of the Royal Navy. The Ministry of Defence argued that the ship is not covered by the Act because it was not in active service, although the *Storaa* was carrying a cargo of steel, including tank tracks, when she sank. The High Court disagreed and ordered the Defence Secretary to reconsider the decision. The ruling could mean that thousands of merchant ships sunk during the two world wars will receive the same protection as the wrecks of warships. More than 4,700 merchant ships were sunk during the First World War and 5,353 during the Second. It is estimated that 35,000 merchant seamen were killed by enemy action, and there are sixteen wrecks in British waters designated war graves, including one German U-boat.

Cartridges from the SS *Storaa* on display at Hastings Museum. (Conrad Hughes, by kind permission of the Shipwreck Heritage Centre, Hastings)

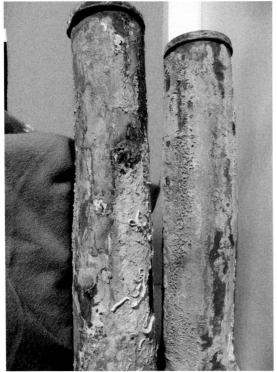

More cartridges from the SS *Storaa* seen at Hastings Museum. (Conrad Hughes, by kind permission of the Shipwreck Heritage Centre, Hastings)

Nine

ORANGES, APPLES, LEMONS AND PINEAPPLES

ALTHOUGH IT is very sad to hear of the loss of a ship, especially where there has also been loss of life, sometimes there is also a more humorous story bringing an unexpected lucky windfall to the local inhabitants, who were never slow to take advantage of the situation. In this chapter I have highlighted ships carrying a cargo of fruit.

Our first ship, the brig *Two Brothers*, came to grief on 1 November 1790 when she was wrecked off Birling Gap. Thankfully, her entire crew were saved but her cargo of lemons was lost. Many thousands of lemons were washed ashore and the local residents, always on hand to pick up the spoils, sold them for 2s (10p) per 100. No doubt that at Christmas there was plenty of homemade lemonade for the children and lemon tarts and lemon cakes for all to enjoy.

Another ship depositing her cargo at Birling Gap was a British sailing vessel that left Jersey in November 1824. She has been reported in various sources as the *Juno, June* or *Jemo*, but to avoid confusion I will refer to her as the *Juno*, and it is only thanks to the bravery of Lieutenant Joseph Clark of the Coast Blockade and his crew that there was no loss of life. The 'Coast Blockade' was a naval force introduced to help fight the increase in smuggling in the nineteenth century, but one of their functions was also to save lives. Under the command of her master Francis Le Fevre and her crew of five, the *Juno* was en route from Jersey to Leith in Glasgow with 1,600 bushels of apples on board (1 bushel being equivalent to approx 25kg) when she hit a horrendous storm coming through the English Channel. By Thursday 18 November she was driven ashore at Birling Gap, presumably whilst trying to reach the shelter of Newhaven harbour. Lieutenant Clark was on duty at the time and saw the vessel in trouble and, although only having been at the station for a matter of weeks, wasted no time in gathering eight men together. Under his guidance they put to sea, risking their own lives in extremely hazardous conditions. Fortunately their actions were not in vain and they rescued the crew. For their gallant efforts, Lieutenant Clark R.N. was presented with a gold medal and each of his men received two sovereigns (£2). On this occasion some of the cargo was also salvaged, and the Customs at Newhaven were able to sell 1,200 bushels of the apples at auction. No doubt the delicious aroma of cooked apples wafted through the area for several days, and the children enjoyed the extra treat as residents took advantage of their unexpected windfall.

Over two decades later, the *Helen* presented the folk along the coast with another unexpected windfall. The master of the *Helen* was a man called William Thom, but when she set sail from St Michael's in Cornwall for London with a cargo of £400 worth of oranges, her sailing captain was a man called Mathews who took to sea with a crew of three and a boy. On Monday 13 January 1840 the *Helen* ran into a terrible storm coming up the Channel and lost her mast. Fortunately by midday the following day, the *Elizabeth Walker* of Glasgow came upon the scene and was able to give the crew a spar for a jury-mast, a temporary mast rigged to replace the broken one. Five days later she had covered a distance of some 800 miles, but on the morning of Tuesday 21 January, whilst off the coast of Worthing, the weather began to worsen from the south-west and caused the crew to reef part of the mainsail. However whilst doing this it tore into three pieces but, thanks to the quick actions of the crew, it was quickly replaced by a jib sheet, a rope or line, used to control the movable corners of the sail. Unfortunately this was not sufficient and, with the gale increasing, the *Helen* found herself drifting ever closer to the rocks at Newhaven. At 9a.m. she dropped anchor half a mile offshore, east of the harbour, to prevent her from drifting any further. With the anchor holding firm the crew were confident that they could ride out the storm, and, although they were so close to land and could see lights that they assumed were a signal to help prevent ships from running ashore, they had no way of attracting attention. By 7p.m. the *Helen* found herself on an ebbing tide, and the water beneath her decreased at an alarming rate until she struck the seabed, rising and falling in the storm. In a short space of time the vessel's cabin was full of water and Captain Mathews decided to cut the anchor cable and allow the vessel to drift ashore near the Buckle Inn at Seaford. Once the vessel was ashore, a crowd of around 1,000 spectators gathered to watch the crew tie a rope to a buoy, whilst they secured the end of the rope to enable the crew to come ashore. No sooner had the last man reached land than the sea smashed the vessel to pieces. The vessel's mate was obviously a lucky man, as he told the gathering crowd, 'I have been fourteen times to St Michael's and wrecked three times in two years, and this is the first time I have lost everything but what I have on.'

Unknown to the *Helen* there had been much activity taking place on shore while she was still drifting towards Newhaven. Earlier that morning she had been sighted off the coast at Rottingdean, with her broken mast and damaged rigging, by Captain Marsh of the coastguards who was concerned for the vessel and gave the order for a boat, ropes and a small gun to be taken to the beach in case it ran aground. A boat was mounted on a small carriage, the equipment loaded, and Captain Marsh and his men pulled it along the beach at the same speed as the *Helen* was drifting, so it remained opposite her at all times. Eventually they arrived at Newhaven harbour pier where they put the boat into the river, crossed to the other side and carried it on their shoulders across the land belonging to Mr Catt, finally arriving at 10a.m. at the beach to find that a large number of spectators had gathered. There they waited for the *Helen* to run aground. The following morning, as the *Helen* broke into pieces by the action of the sea, large numbers of the locals, as far east as Cuckmere, were busy collecting the cargo of oranges that was being washed ashore. That afternoon 100 oranges were being sold in Alfriston for 2s (10p) and there were also sightings of oranges being loaded by the sack on to carts to be taken to Brighton. There was no doubt that plenty of fresh oranges were enjoyed that week and those that could not be eaten were probably turned into marmalade.

Thirty-two years later it was tinned pineapples the locals could enjoy. They were aboard the *Union*, sometimes referred to as the *American Union*, that left New York on Friday 22 November 1872 bound for London, under the command of her master named Delano and his crew of twenty-six. She had a mixed cargo of sewing machines and barrels of lampblack (a type of carbon black obtained from the soot of burned fat, oil, tar and resin). This was used as a pigment, and as reinforcement in rubber goods, or as a black pigment in cements, ceramics, shoe polishes, etc. Also on board were toys, wheat, flour and the mentioned tins of pineapple. The voyage went smoothly until the vessel reached the English Channel, and during the evening of Monday 16 December she found herself off Newhaven in a strong south-westerly wind, but as she was under little sail her master was not too concerned as, despite the extremely poor visibility, he still believed she was in mid-Channel and nowhere near the notorious rocks. The lookout first spotted land and, as she was still under sail, the order was given for more sail with the intension to tack and sail out to sea away from the shoreline and danger. Unfortunately she was too close and the crew had left it too late. Before anything could be done for the *Union* she ran aground opposite the Blatchington Coastguard Station and rolled onto her broadside with the deck facing the sea. Meanwhile the coastguard watch at Blatchington had seen that the vessel was too close to the shore and had informed Mr Scott, the officer in charge, who mustered his men and they gathered up the rocket apparatus and were quickly on the scene. A line was fixed to the *Union*, and sixteen men were brought ashore using the line and a basket. The remainder of the crew stayed with the vessel until finally the ebbing tide left her high and dry, allowing them to walk ashore safely. After being looked after at the Blatchington Coastguard Station arrangements were made for the crew to be transferred to the American Consul in London.

By midday the returning tide, helped by the strong wind, started to break up the vessel, which had been insured for £8,000, but it was obvious that the vessel and its contents had been grossly underinsured, and very soon £25,000-worth of cargo was strewn along the beaches at Seaford. Some of the barrels containing the flour and lampblack burst open causing a huge black cloud to drift inland on the wind. By now a large crowd, including officials who were there to try and collect and protect the cargo, had gathered on the beach and very soon found themselves covered in black from head to toe! The black cloud drifted further inland for a couple of miles and even blackened a whole flock of sheep!

The next day men were employed to salvage anything of value from the wreck, including the copper from the hull, as it was estimated that one more high tide would completely destroy the vessel. For two hours the team worked frantically, battling with the incoming tide, whilst others, legally or illegally, were engaged in recovering the cargo that had been washed up. The shoreline, some said, resembled an open market with barrels of flour, resin, boxes of cloth pegs, timber, sewing machines, brooms, casks of lampblack, tobacco leaf, toys, tins of pineapple and casks of biscuits laid out on display for all to view, and no doubt sample. Although some of the barrels remained intact, the majority had been broken open, including the largest part of the cargo consisting of wheat which was entirely lost because the sea caused the wheat to swell, so bursting the bags open. The wheat sank to the bottom of the sea leaving a layer several metres thick, clearly visible at low tide. The cargo was taken to a yard at the Royal Artillery Battery and to enable it to be transported quickly every horse and cart in the area was requisitioned from the locals, who did not mind as the extra income would come in very handy as it was Christmastime. Another bonus for the people of Seaford was the sewing machines; no doubt some found their way to the housewives as a surprise gift, whilst the children found the odd extra toy in their Christmas stocking. Many a table that Christmas served up a most generous helping of tinned pineapples and some of the older residents can even remember their grandparents talking about it.

Five years later the unexpected 'gift' was a very large cargo, 3,560 boxes in all, of oranges from Seville bound for Leith in Glasgow. On 26 November 1877 the steamship *Mizpah* left Seville with her master Henry George Cram and his crew of twelve men and arrived off Portland at 11a.m. on Wednesday 5 December and dropped anchor for a short while before continuing her journey, around 3.30p.m., up the English Channel. What happened next to the *Mizpah* is not clear because, at around 4.30a.m. the following morning, the only survivor, twenty-year-old steward William Page, had left his berth and gone to the galley to make coffee for his fellow officers. Half an hour later he heard the mate shout 'Hard-a-port', quickly followed by a collision. It appears that the *Mizpah* had been struck on her port bow in thick fog and a force 6 south-westerly gale by an unknown sailing vessel that had no lights. The damage to the *Mizpah* was so severe that, as she was taking in water, the master ordered the engineer to get the pumps working quickly. However, this became impossible as the water had already got into the engine room and extinguished the boilers. The collision had also carried away the *Mizpah*'s lifeboat, so the master gave the order to ready the punt, a small 14ft boat, as the *Mizpah* was rapidly sinking. Seven hands, including Page, got on board whilst the master, first mate, and four of the crew lowered the punt but, in the panic, the crew inside it failed to hand the rope attached to the front of the boat to the master. Once in the sea the punt moved away swiftly from the *Mizpah*, so that the master and the other crew members could not get into it. Once the error was spotted, the crew in the punt tried to turn back to collect the others, but discovered that they only had one oar on board. Within twenty minutes the *Mizpah*'s bow rose up and the vessel went down stern first, taking with her the master, First Mate John Thomas Bryant, First Engineer Nicholl Gavangh, Able Seaman J. Cram (who was the master's brother), W. Bell and another unknown sailor.

With the sole oar the second mate Thomas Lewis steered the punt before the wind for three hours and we can only imagine how they must have felt, unable to help and losing their colleagues to the sea. Finally they saw what they believed was the Royal Sovereign light but, as dawn broke, they realised it was the Beachy Head light and the cliffs with the awesome surf breaking along the shore line. On board they discussed if they should run for shore through the surf or stay offshore and wait for help to come. They decided to risk running for shore, but when they were 100 yards from the beach, the punt went broadside to the waves, throwing all seven men into the raging sea as the boat capsized. The action of the surf soon washed everyone ashore but the only man to survive the ordeal was William Page, who had been given a lifebelt by the master just before the punt was launched.

At 8.30a.m. Henry John Cooke, on lookout duty at Cuckmere Coastguard Station, saw the upturned punt and immediately informed John Heather, the officer in charge. With the aid of his telescope, he could see a body lying in the surf, so he mustered his men and they made their way to the beach and found Page, almost naked, crawling on his hands and knees up the shingle beach in driving sleet and rain. Two of the coastguards rushed to drag him clear of the water and carried him to Heather's home to be treated for exhaustion and exposure. The other coastguards recovered the punt, a chronometer and the *Mizpah*'s cash-box.

The six men in the punt with William Page were: the second mate, Thomas Lewis, aged forty-two, from London; Able Seaman James Pooley, aged thirty, from Ipswich; Able Seaman Patrick Law, aged twenty-seven, from Newcastle; Second Engineer Charles Sbensfan, from Stockholm; Fireman Edward Hall, aged eighteen, from Newport; and the Engineer's Steward Charles Thomas, aged fifteen, from Bristol. It is clear that William Page and Charles Thomas had become close friends whilst on board because, over Friday night, Page had become delirious and was asking after his shipmates, in particular Thomas.

During Thursday and Friday the bodies of five of the men from the punt were recovered from along the shoreline between Birling Gap and Seaford. The second mate, Thomas Lewis, left a wife and five children, and his wife travelled to Seaford on 9 December to take her husband's body home. A local collection was arranged by Mr Sargent of The Shipwrecked Mariners' Society and £10 was raised to help her pay for his body to be returned. He must have be a very compassionate man because he also

The SS *Indiana* going down on the West Sussex coast. (By kind permission of West Sussex County Council Library Service)

arranged for the carriage of the body to the railway station for a nominal charge of 2s 6d (12½p) instead of the usual cost of £3. At the inquest, Mr Atkins, the part owner of the *Mizpah*, revealed that only about a month earlier the *Mizpah*, under the command of Henry George Cram, had been caught in a gale when sailing from Swansea to Seville and ended up 200 miles off course in the Atlantic Ocean.

Another cargo of oranges, this time from the steamship *Indiana*, ended up covering the beach at Worthing on 1 March 1901 when she was wrecked near the Half Brick Inn at East Worthing, after colliding, in thick fog, with the German cross-Atlantic *steamer City of Washington*, which was on her way to New York.

The story begins on 28 February when the large oil steamer *City of Washington* got into difficulties near the Owers Lightship around 9 miles south-south-east of Selsey Bill and decided to proceed slowly down the Channel. Meanwhile the *Indiana* was sailing to London from Venice via Valencia with a cargo of oranges and lemons. She hit thick fog and was inching her way up the Channel, when at around 5p.m. the *City of Washington* ran into her hitting her amidships. The *Indiana* was badly damaged, so the *City of Washington* took on board the crew but, as she appeared to be still seaworthy, the crew decided to return to her. However, the weather took a turn for the worse and finally the hawser snapped but, after several hours, the ship was still afloat when the London tug *Simla* came alongside. She took the *Indiana* in tow, but the stricken ship began listing heavily and finally ground to a halt 1 mile south of Worthing Pier and the tug decided to take the crew to Newhaven. Eventually the cargo of oranges and lemons was washed ashore in their thousands and ended up as far as Goring and along to Rottingdean. Large quantities were picked by the local residents who either ate them or took them home to make marmalade. Stallholders also arrived with baskets and sacks and by the time the salvage boat turned up the following day, the beach was clean. One beachcomber lost his life when he was bowled over by a wave after wading into the sea to grab more fruit.

The local coastguards tried to take possession of cases that were being washed up unopened, but the gatherers on the beach had almost turned themselves into a fighting mob. The wreck of the *Indiana*, now known as the 'Orange Wreck', rested in 40ft of water, but because the wreck was a hazard to other shipping, it was later blown up, although it is now beginning to emerge and some of its ribs are sticking out of the sand, and a bathroom, complete with taps and a wash basin are exposed.

A picture board detailing the wreck can be seen near Worthing Pier. To mark the sinking of the 1,000-ton SS *Indiana*, each March an annual fruit-flinging contest is held usually on the beach. Artefacts from the *Indiana* can be seen at Marlipins Museum at Shoreham and include the ship's steam whistle, and some of the oranges and lemons washed ashore, whilst Worthing Museum has the hub of her wheel and a rim from one of her portholes.

Oranges and lemons collected from the shore when they washed up after the wreck of the "**SS Indiana**" in March 1901.

Oranges and lemons, preserved at the Marlipins Museum, Shoreham, which were collected from the shore when they washed up after the wrecking of the SS *Indiana* in March 1901. (Conrad Hughes, by kind permission of Marlipins Museum, Shoreham-by-Sea)

A bucket clearly displaying the name *Indiana*, recovered from the wreck. (Conrad Hughes, by kind permission of Marlipins Museum, Shoreham-by-Sea)

The *Indiana*'s steam whistle, also recovered from the wreck. (Conrad Hughes, by kind permission of Marlipins Museum, Shoreham-by-Sea)

Spectators gathering the oranges and lemons that covered Worthing beach when the *Indiana* was wrecked. (By kind permission of Worthing Library)

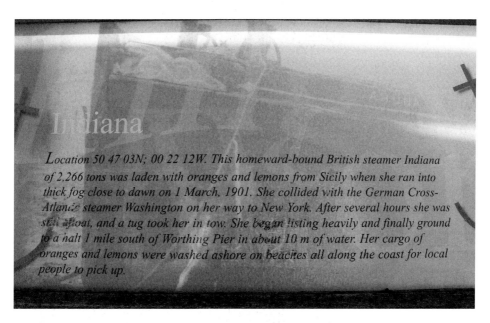

Location 50 47 03N; 00 22 12W. This homeward-bound British steamer Indiana of 2,266 tons was laden with oranges and lemons from Sicily when she ran into thick fog close to dawn on 1 March, 1901. She collided with the German Cross-Atlantic steamer Washington on her way to New York. After several hours she was still afloat, and a tug took her in tow. She began listing heavily and finally ground to a halt 1 mile south of Worthing Pier in about 10 m of water. Her cargo of oranges and lemons were washed ashore on beaches all along the coast for local people to pick up.

Story board near to Worthing Pier telling the story of the *Indiana*. (Conrad Hughes)

Ten

LOST, FOUND, UNKNOWN, BUT NOT FORGOTTEN

WITH MORE people turning to diving as a leisure interest, we are finding more wrecked ships that were known and lost, some completely unknown, and some that were forgotten and are now beginning to reveal their secrets. In this chapter a few are highlighted.

The first ship in this section is the *Thomas Lawrence*, an eighteenth-century Danish schooner that was known to have sunk off Hastings in 1862, and has become known as the 'Tombstone Wreck', because a tombstone recovered from the wreck has helped to identify it.

The site was discovered by divers in 1983, and later researched by Dr Peter Marsden, of the Shipwreck and Coastal Heritage Centre, and excavated by Wessex Archaeology. The wreck is now owned by the Nautical Museums Trust and was transferred in writing by Torben Broberg, a direct descendant of the original owner. At the time she was wrecked, the *Thomas Lawrence* was carrying a large cargo of interesting items, including fifty wooden boxes, each containing twenty flintlock front-loading muskets. Some boxes contained bottles of the square Dutch type, marked with the words 'de Cuiper'. Two boxes contained a variety of items including iron chains, perfume bottles, cheap jewellery, and twisted glass rings. Some of these finds can be seen at Hastings Museum and also in the museum is the more interesting tombstone recovered from the ship. Although it is the tombstone of a Danish family, strangely the stone is inscribed in English:

> Here repose the mortal remains of Julia Adriane Jahncke, born Beverboudt, born in St Croix the 7th February 1827. Died in St Thomas the 6 March 1858. Franz Friedrich Jahncke born 6 March 1858 died the 19 March 1858.

A rare photograph of the *Thomas Lawrence* before she was lost. (By kind permission of the Shipwreck Heritage Centre, Hastings)

The tombstone of Julia Adriane Jahncke and her young son Franz, which was being shipped to the Danish Virgin Islands and is now on display at the Shipwreck and Heritage Centre, Hastings, led to the identification of the wreck of the *Thomas Lawrence*. (Conrad Hughes, by kind permission of the Shipwreck Heritage Centre, Hastings)

One of a number of machetes found on board the *Thomas Lawrence*. These were to be used for cutting sugar cane in the West Indies. (Conrad Hughes, by kind permission of the Shipwreck and Heritage Centre, Hastings)

Julia was thirty-one and had died in childbirth, and little Franz died thirteen days later. It would appear that Mr Jahncke now wished 'to tidy matters' before remarrying and was sending the tombstone out to the Danish Virgin Islands as his wife and child were buried in an unmarked grave.

It would seem from records that the *Thomas Lawrence*, a wooden schooner, was ordered by Christian August Broberg, a rich Copenhagen ship owner and coffee trader, and was built around 1838–39 in Lulea, northern Sweden. The name of the ship, *Thomas Lawrence*, has an interesting story too, and is thought that she was named because at the time Jens Wolff, the Danish Consul in London, was a relation of Mrs Broberg, and Wolff's English wife Isabella had an affair with the painter Thomas Lawrence, after he painted her portrait in 1803.

According to Lloyd's List the *Thomas Lawrence* left Hamburg in 1862 and was bound for Haiti with a stop at Charlotte Amalie on St Thomas in the Danish (now American) Virgin Islands to unload a tombstone. Also on board was a crate of machetes and as these were commonly used for cutting sugar cane in the West Indies, including St Thomas, we can only surmise that was their destination. There were also crates of old flintlock muskets and it has been suggested that because of their poor condition these weapons were cheap and perhaps destined for Haiti where they would have been sought after by the various groups involved in the power struggles of the time. Lloyd's List also reports that the *Thomas Lawrence* was rammed amidships on the port side by the German steamer *Die Schwalbe* at 3a.m. on 10 March 1862 and sank with the loss of the ship's master Captain Poulsen.

As you can image, with so many ships wrecked at Seaford, most of the wreckage has now become a complete jumble on the seabed, with items from one wreck tangled with another. However there are a group of items that must have come from an as yet unnamed big ship. They sit in line with the last groyne to the east of the Martello Tower near to the first two of the Seven Sisters. There is an enormous anchor which has been nicknamed by local divers as 'the Roman Anchor'. It has a 12ft shaft and a ring on the end, approximately 2ft in diameter, with one of the huge iron flukes buried in the seabed. For now, where this ship came from remains a mystery, but it looks large enough to hold a ship that would have been the size of the HMS *Victory*. Of course

One of several crates of old flintlock muskets that were possibly destined for Haiti to use in the various power struggles at the time. (Conrad Hughes, by kind permission of the Shipwreck and Heritage Centre, Hastings)

Various perfume and cosmetics bottles from Paris found on board the *Thomas Lawrence*. (Conrad Hughes, by kind permission of the Shipwreck and Heritage Centre, Hastings)

Numerous bottles were found on the wreck, including the square-shaped Dutch bottles, marked with the words 'de Cuiper'. (Conrad Hughes, by kind permission of the Shipwreck and Heritage Centre, Hastings)

Patterned plates and some of the numerous bottles recovered on the ship which has become known as the Bottle Ship. (Conrad Hughes, by kind permission of Littlehampton Museum)

a ship can lose an anchor without being wrecked, but further evidence of a wrecked ship has been found including large pieces of oak up to 5ft in length and bronze pins, some 2½in in diameter. Elm deadeyes have also been discovered in the same area, and these have iron banding around them, and again can be compared in size with those on HMS *Victory*. Divers have also found cannon, so far three 32-pounders and two 24-pounders as well as a long bow-chaser, like those used for ranging shots. Between the Martello Tower and Seaford Head divers have also discovered a vast yard – a long spar that supports the head of a square sail. It is 28ft long and on each end are wheels 5in in diameter for ropes that would have been at least ½in thick and used to swivel the yards. The yard, together with other big timber work, lies at the foot of a large gully running out to sea and is now half-covered in silt. Perhaps one day divers will discover something that will identify this ship.

An unnamed ship was wrecked near Littlehampton sometime in the nineteenth century, and has become known as the 'Bottle Ship', because her cargo included a vast number of bottles of porter. It would appear that she was a wooden merchant sailing ship which would have had two or possibly three masts. It is carved from oak and is held together with nails and copper alloy bolts with the outer hull copper-sheathed. It appears that the Bottle Ship was carrying a general cargo which included pottery, cutlery, razors, guns and lengths of cast-iron pipes. These are clearly visible on the seabed, and in 1983 divers counted at least 204 pipes, and by their appearance is has been suggested that they were designed as water or drainage pipes. To the area aft of the pipes are five different types of pottery: blue and white transfer-printed willow-pattern plates with the maker Read and Clementson marked on them; pink, blue and black transfer-printed ware of an unknown pattern; dark brown transfer-printed ware; annular ware with mocha pattern and some refined plain white ware.

Unknown quantities of cutlery that included spoons, knives and forks have been raised from the sea. A number of the fiddle-pattern spoons that were popular in the nineteenth century, and bone-handled knives are preserved in Littlehampton Museum. The other interesting items include gun flints and flintlocks, glass salt cellars, silver sugar tongs and cutthroat razors. Intriguingly, the bone handles of the razors are engraved with a number of different patterns that include portraits of George Washington, the Liberty Bell and some rural farming scenes, and a razor handle at Littlehampton Museum is engraved with a horizontal wave pattern. Interestingly the design on the willow pattern crockery gives a clue to the dating of the wreck as this pattern was only used between 1833 and 1835, but for now the name of the ship is lost to the depths of the sea.

The beer bottles and barrels were found in front of the pipes. Two barrels, probably hogsheads containing around 54 gallons of ale or porter, were excavated in 1983 and have the name 'Barclay and Perkins' burnt onto the lids. This particular brewery was founded in 1781 at Southwark in London and was the largest producer of exported beer during the nineteenth century. The broken beer bottles were scattered on the seabed in the bow area. In 1983 around 500 complete and corked bottles, of the typical

Label from a bottle of Bottle
Wreck Porter, available
from September to March.
(By kind permission of
Hammerpot Brewery)

'porter' shape, which was common between 1760 and 1918, half a pint in size, were
raised from the seabed. Some of the bottle corks were inscribed 'Kinnley Williams,
London', but brewers by this name could not be traced. The bottles contained porter
made from very dark ale based on roasted malt, a type that was very popular in the
eighteenth century and known as the 'working class beer'. Samples of yeast preserved
in some of the corked bottles was used to recreate the original beer in 1991 and sold
as flag porter by the Darwin Brewery in the UK. In 2007, the local Hammerpot
Brewery produced a 'Hammerpot Bottle Wreck Porter', which has become very
successful. It is produced in 9-gallon firkins and also in bottles and available from
September to March.

Appendix I

TYPES OF SHIPS, RIGGING AND SAILS

Barge — A flat-bottomed coastal trader with leeboards each side to prevent the vessel making leeway.

Barque — A sailing vessel that has three or more masts, whose sails are mainly square.

Boeier — A type of Dutch barge-yacht with leeboards. If the seas are high and the boeier gets into trouble, the leeboards tend to bang about forming an obstruction which can prevent another vessel (i.e. a lifeboat) from coming alongside.

Brigitane — A two-masted vessel, squared rigged on both masts.

Dandy (sailing) — A sailing vessel with two masts; a small mizzen is aft of the rudderpost.

Fore and aft — The vessel's sails are set parallel, or close to, the fore and aft centre line of the vessel.

Jib — A triangular sail that is set before the foremast, that does not overlap the main sail.

Jury rig — Temporary makeshift mast and sails rigged after a ship has become disabled.

Galley punt — Small 21–30ft sailing craft with lug sails, approximately amidships, carrying a crew of three or four.

Ketch — Two-masted vessel, the smaller of the masts placed behind the larger, and in front of the stern.

Lugger — Large boat, often 40ft by 13ft, with two mast-carrying lugsails. They have little cabin space but usually some forward shelter.

Mainsail — The sail attached to the main, or largest, mast of the boat.

Mizzen mast — The third mast on a ship with three or more masts, the third mast

	from the front. The rear mast on a boat such as a ketch or yawl, or the mast nearest to the back.
Rigging	All lines, shrouds, and stays on a boat that pertain to the sail and mast.
Schooner	A vessel with two or more masts, the main mast set aft the smaller mast.
Shroud	A wire cable used as standing on the permanent rigging to support the mast.
Spritsails	Sails that are held up by a spar or sprit from the base of the mast to peak of the sail.
Yawl	Two-masted boat with the smaller after mast stepped behind the stern post.

Appendix II

NAUTICAL TERMS

Aft	The back of the boat, behind the mast.
Aground	When the hull or keel of the vessel touches the bottom.
Amidships	In the centre of the boat.
Anemometer	An instrument that measures the velocity of the wind.
Astern	To the rear of the boat.
Ballast	Heavy material placed in the bottom of a ship to give stability.
Batten down	Close and make secure all openings of a vessel, especially the deck.
Beam ends	A boat is said to be on her 'beam ends' when she has heeled over so far that her deck beams for almost vertical.
Before the wind	Sailing with the wind coming from behind.
Boom	The bar to which the boom, or foot, of the sail is attached.
Bow	The front end of a vessel.
Bowsprit	The spar extending forwards from the bow, usually horizontal and on which the sails of the ship are attached.
Breeches buoy	This is a piece of rescue equipment. A line is connected between the rescuers and the shipwreck, and a seat in the form of a pair of leather shorts is suspended from the line, and pulled along.
Chock	A piece of timber which supports the long boat on the deck.
Ensign	A flag identifying the nationality of the ship.
Furl	To roll a sail up and secure it to yard or boom.
Galley	A ship's kitchen.
Helm	The rudder and the tiller or wheel, used to steer the ship.
Hoist	To haul up, to raise the sail.
Hull	The body of the boat.

Jolly boat	Traditionally the term refers to a boat carried by a ship, powered by four or six oars and occasionally yawl-rigged sails.
Leeward	Downwind. The side of the vessel away from which the wind is blowing, which therefore provides protection from the wind.
Lifeline	A safety device that consists of lines on posts or stanchions around the deck of a ship.
Neap tide	The lowest tide in the lunar month. The high tides are lower than mean high, and the low tides are lower than mean low.
Pintle	A pin or bolt used as a vertical pivot or hinge on a rudder.
Port	The left side of the ship.
Rudder	A board which is mounted beneath the water at or near to the rear of the boat and is used for steering.
Starboard	The right side of the ship.
Stern	The trailing end of the vessel.
Stow	To put something in its place. To store.
Tacking	When a ship is sailed on a zig-zag course staying as close as possible to the wind, so that the wind comes over the vessel from alternate sides.
Tiller	The spar by which the rudder is controlled.
Winch	A device for hauling in lines.
Yawing	Swinging from side to side.

BIBLIOGRAPHY

Books

Thomas, R., *Interesting and Authentic Narratives of the Most Remarkable Shipwrecks, Fires, Famines, Calamities, Providential Deliverances and Lamentable Disaster* (General Books, 1837 – reprinted 2000)

Odam, J., with Chapman, B., *The Seaford Story 1000–2000 AD* (S.B. Publications, 1999)

Cheal, H. (junior), *The Ships and Mariners of Shoreham* (Country Books, 2009)

Prothero, R.E. (ed.), *Works of Lord Byron, Letters and Journals Vol. 1* (John Murray, 1894–1904)

Elleray, D.R., *A Millennium Encyclopaedia of Worthing History* (Optimus Books, 1998)

Berry, P. and Longstaff-Tyrrell, P., *Aspects of Alfriston* (S.B. Publications, 2006)

Marsden, P., *Guide to the Wreck Site of the 'Amsterdam' 1749 at Hastings* (Hastings Borough Council, 2007)

Blann, R., *A Town's Pride – Victorian Lifeboatmen and their Community* (Rob Blann, 1990)

Thornton, N., *Sussex Shipwrecks* (Countryside Books, 1988)

Hutchinson, G., *Mary Stanford Disaster – The Story of a Lifeboat – November 15 1928*

McDonald, K., *Dive Sussex* (Underwater World Publications, 1999)

Renno, D., *East Sussex Shipwrecks of the 19th Century (Pevensey–Hastings–Rye)* (Book Guild Ltd, 2002)

Renno, D., *Beachy Head Shipwrecks of the 19th Century (Pevensey–Eastbourne–Newhaven)* (Amherst Publishing Ltd, 2004) (www.shipwrecksofsussex.co.uk)

Surtees, J., *Beachy Head* (S.B. Publications, 1997)

Armstrong, R., *The Battle of Beachy Head*

Biggs, H., *The Sound of Maroons: Story of Life Saving Services on the Kent and Sussex Coasts* (Terence Dalton, 1977)

Larn, R. and Larn, B., *Shipwreck Index of the British Isles – Vol. 2* (Tor Mark Press, 1995)

Morris, J., *The Story of the Selsey Lifeboats* (1994)

Morris, J., *The Story of the Eastbourne Lifeboats* (1994)

Newspapers

Various copies of the following newspapers dating from 1747 to 1998:

The Argus
Sussex Weekly Advertiser
Hastings and St Leonards News
Hastings and St Leonards Chronicle
Hastings and St Leonards Independent
Hastings and St Leonards News
Hastings and St Leonards Observer
South Eastern Advertiser
Sussex County magazine
Sussex Life
Sussex Express
Seaford Gazette
Sussex Daily News
Eastbourne Chronicle
Eastbourne Gazette
Eastbourne Standard

Museums to visit

Newhaven Local and Maritime Museum – www.newhavenmuseum.co.uk
Seaford Museum and Heritage Society – www.seafordmuseum.co.uk
Shipwreck Heritage Museum, Hastings – http://shipwreck-heritage.org.uk
Marlipins Museum, Shoreham-by-Sea – http://marlipins.adur.org.uk

Websites

Amsterdam Wreck Site – http://shipwreck-heritage.org.uk
www.coastguardsofyesteryear.org
www.dive125.co.uk
www.westsussexpast.org.uk
Jan Letten – www.wrecksite.eu
Hammerpot Brewery – www.hammerpot-brewery.co.uk
Wessex Archaeology – www.wessexarch.co.uk

INDEX